G. A. Bredero

The Spanish Brabanter

medieval & renaissance texts & studies

VOLUME II

G. A. Bredero

The Spanish Brabanter

A Seventeenth-Century
Dutch Social Satire
In Five Acts

Translated by

H. David Brumble III

medieval & renaissance texts & studies
Center for Medieval & Early Renaissance Studies
Binghamton, New York
1982

The Foundation for the Promotion of the
Translation of Dutch Literary Works (*Stichting ter
bevordering van de vertaling van Nederlands
letterkundig werk*) has generously provided a grant
to assist with publication costs.

Center for Medieval and Early Renaissance Studies
State University of New York at Binghamton
Binghamton, New York

Library of Congress Cataloging in Publication Data

Bredero, G. A. (Gerbrand Adriaenszoon), 1585-1618.
    The Spanish Brabanter.

    (Medieval & Renaissance texts & studies; 11)
    Translation of: Spaanschen Brabander.
    I. Brumble, H. David. II. Title. III. Series.
PT5610.S613   1981   839.3'123   81-19004
ISBN 0-86698-018-0   AACR2

Printed in the United States of America

For Lizzie

Contents

Acknowledgements

One of the good things about this profession of scholarship is the spirit which moves people like Paul Sellin, William Z. Shetter, and Hermine J. van Nuis to take the time to read through a book-length manuscript written up by a man they do not know. Though under no bond of friendship, they took considerable pains to make me wiser and this book better than it would otherwise have been. In my own department this same spirit — combined, I hope, with friendship — brought me the help of Walt Evert, Bob Gale, Michael Helfand, Philip Smith, and Michael West. I would also like to thank Mario DiCesare, Director and General Editor of Medieval and Renaissance Texts and Studies, for his careful and considerate treatment of Bredero, Brabanter, and me. Finally, I wish to express my gratitude for the National Endowment for the Humanities Younger Humanist Fellowship and the University of Pittsburgh Faculty Grant which provided the material assistance so necessary to such projects as this.

H. DAVID BRUMBLE III

University of Pittsburgh
September, 1981

G. A. Bredero

The Spanish Brabanter

Fig. 1. Jan Steen, The Meeting of the Rhetoricians.
Copyright Bibliothèque royale Albert Ier, Bruxelles.

Introduction

Gerbrand Adriaensz Bredero's *The Spanish Brabanter* (1617),
if not the greatest play ever written in the Netherlands, is
perhaps the most beloved. In this play more than in any of his
other works, Bredero embodies the essence of early Amsterdam, a city he brings before us ringing with talk, with selling,
with bawdry; a city stretching to accommodate a flood of immigration and equal floods of controversy; a city at once
uneasy with and accepting of its startling diversity; a city
whose river flows foul; a city where Dürers and Holbeins are
offered casually as items for sale; a city alive. Bredero was
quite in harmony with the city he depicted—he created pro-
digally, sketching a halt-legged beadle, drinking contests, a
fop, beggars, gabby old men, marble-playing boys, a roguish
servant lad, hacklers, spinsters, a goldsmith, a notary, a bribe-
taking sheriff, ladies of the night, junk dealers, the plague,
widows, bakers, eel hawkers, and bankrupts. Bredero mounts
on the stage the same kind of breathing verisimilitude we
find—without the need for translation—in the canvases of
Frans Hals and Jan Steen.

Such fond regard for Bredero's time-shrinking dramatiza-
tions of Amsterdam is of long standing in the Netherlands. As
early as 1694 Casparus Commelin, Regent of the Oudezijds
Almshouse, wrote:

> Beyond all doubt [Bredero] managed to do for the
> spectators and audiences of Amsterdam what
> Terence had done for them in Rome. There are old
> people today who testify that whenever they see the
> play or hear it read, they at once feel fifty years
> younger and in the Fish Hall or the poultry and fish
> market, hearing the shouts of the old sales
> women. . . .[1]

Anyone in our own day who is interested to hear the shouts that echoed to the scenes of Hals, Steen, and Rembrandt can hardly do better than to hear Bredero.

Bredero himself was born in 1585, in the heart of Amsterdam's thriving middle class. His mother, Mary Gerbrand, was of good family, her brothers having made their way to moderate fortune by acting as estate brokers — and as brokers for the cloisters which were falling victim to the rise of official Calvinism. Bredero's father, Adriaen Cornelisz, was a shoemaker; less ambiguously it might be said that he was a shoe manufacturer. So far was his income above that of a mere cobbler that he was able to invest in the wave of construction which swept Amsterdam in his generation. He made a moderate fortune.[2] He was also elected to a captaincy in the city militia, a post of some local prestige.

Mary and Adriaen provided their son with a good education. The boy learned English and French, the latter well enough to write a bit of poetry in French. While Bredero admits to no Latin and less Greek, he did know the classics well enough in 1611 to write a letter in which he quotes Thales, Bias of Priene, Periander of Corinth, Cleobulus, Marcus Aurelius, Plautus, Seneca, Solon, and Cicero, along with Solomon and St. Paul for good measure.[3]

Bredero would also have learned a good deal outside his school. For the first seventeen years of his life Bredero lived in a house on the Nes, near Amsterdam's central market place, the Dam. Not only would he there have enjoyed a splendid vantage from which to watch the city's effervescence, he also happened to be living next door to the St. Pieterskapel, which had been converted into a butcher's shop after the Reformation. On the top floor of this building, Amsterdam's then most prominent literary guild held its meetings.[4] This guild, the Eglantine, was one of many such "chambers of rhetoric" (see below) in the Netherlands. Jan Steen provides us with some marvelous views of these chambers, and even some of the Eglantine itself (Steen was a member).[5] As we see these paintings (fig. 1, opposite page 1), as we see the guildsmen at their windows reading their verse to the crowd outside (to the tune of the flagons clanking inside), we must realize that the boy next door could hardly have escaped hearing the verse. Given the man the boy was to become, it is hard to imagine that he did not attend many of the plays that the Eglantine produced in those years above the butcher shop, hard to imagine that the boy did not meet and talk with the poets, amateur actors, painters, and drinkers who were members. Small wonder then that, as Bredero was later to write, he had been attracted since childhood to "lovely poesy" above "the sweetness of all other pastimes."[6]

Despite this early inclination to poetry Bredero began training for a career as a painter shortly after his family moved to a house on the Oudezijds Voorburghwaal, a more expensive neighborhood (1602). His teacher was Frans Badens, known in his day as an Italianate painter. Though none of Badens' paintings have survived, it is known that he painted at least three works on classical subjects: a Venus, a Minerva, and a Juno.[7] I will later discuss the relationship between Bredero's training as a painter and his work as a dramatist, but it should be said here that the principles that guided Rembrandt's teacher, Pieter Lastman, would almost certainly have guided Badens—and his student, Bredero.[8] Unfortunately, none of Bredero's paintings have come down to us either,[9] though an inventory of Adriaen's possessions does contain references to paintings of "David and Abigail," "David and Bathsheba," "Pyramus and Thisbe," and "Dame Fortune," all painted by his son. We can assume that Bredero was a successful painter, at least successful enough to allow him to write in the midsummer of 1613 that self-interest urged him to painting and its "sweet remuneration"—but, as he continued, "poetry brings pleasure,"[10] and so Bredero sacrificed his brushes to his muse.

By the time Bredero wrote this comparison (1613, at the age of twenty-six) he had already written a sizeable body of poetry—pastorals, religious verse, laments, occasional verse, love poetry—and at least four plays, all of which had been successfully performed. Yet his assessment was quite realistic. Netherlandish painters, by painting and engraving for an increasingly broad and moneyed segment of the Dutch populace, could often earn much more than a mere sufficiency. Poets and dramatists simply could not, and this for several reasons. First, while there is evidence that, by contemporary standards, a remarkably high percentage of Netherlanders could read (perhaps fifty percent could have boasted minimal competency, at least in the towns[11]), still the Netherlands had too small a population to support poets by book sales. And the money from book sales went largely or entirely to publishers at any rate. Second, there was no patronage system for the arts, at least not to anything like the extent that such patronage existed in England and Italy at this time. Bredero wrote his flowery dedications to such luminaries as the Swedish ambassador, Jacob van Dyck, but he could not have expected to be much enriched for his flourishes. Even so highly regarded and so long-lived a poet as Joost van den Vondel, who was named the laureate of Dutch poets in 1653, derived his living largely from his hosiery business. In fact, when, at the age of seventy, Vondel was bankrupt by his son's selfish mismanagement of the business, he earned his bread as a clerk in an Amsterdam bank,[12] where he worked as hard as any other clerk until he was well into his eighties.

Finally, perhaps the most important reason why Bredero could not earn his keep as a dramatist is that the theaters were technically closed throughout this period because of official Calvinist disapproval[13] — although performances were allowed for charitable purposes. Amsterdam's Old Men's Home, for example, received some two thousand guilders between July, 1615 and April of 1616 from performances of plays, mostly those of Samuel Coster (a medical doctor) and Bredero.[14] So, while his plays were certainly well attended, this did very little toward Bredero's enrichment. Even so popular a playwright as Jan Vos, who wrote frequently gory, usually spectacular stuff, earned more as a glazier than as a writer. "On the other hand," writes J. L. Price:

> considerable prestige was attached to the writing of
> plays in the styles accepted by the cultured élite. If
> composition of poems was a rich man's hobby, it
> was also one of the few ways by which those lower
> in the social scale could bring themselves to the
> notice of their superiors, and thereby gain in status.
> Joachim Oudaen, a modest tile-maker, could be on
> almost familiar terms with a number of regents of
> his town, Rotterdam, through his poetry and his ac-

tivities as a zealous [member of the local chamber of
rhetoric].[15]

Bredero, the shoemaker's son, must have been delighted
when his poetry gained him an invitation to the salon hosted
by the wealthy and literate Roemer Visscher. There were in-
vitations as well from P. C. Hooft—a learned poet and gover-
nor of Muiden and Gooiland—at his castle. Bredero, the
shoemaker's son, would also have been honored, then, when
he was asked to join the Eglantine (probably in 1611[16]), where
he could become a guild brother of Hooft, Visscher, and
Samuel Coster, and many others. Bredero's association with
these men and with the Eglantine was important to him for
other reasons as well. In order to get a fuller sense of what the
chamber meant to Bredero as a dramatist, it will be worth our
while to pause for a brief survey of the traditions of the
chambers.

The Chambers of Rhetoric

At least as early as the fourteenth century there existed in
the Netherlands—as in Spain, France, and Italy[17]—semi-
religious organizations whose members were responsible for
the production of the mystery and miracle plays. In the
Netherlands these companies evolved into literary societies
with marvelous names: the Eyes of Christ was founded at
Diest in 1302, the Alpha and Omega in 1398 at Ypres, the Holy
Ghost in 1428 at Brugge, the Jesus with the Balsam in 1428 at
Ghent, and the Marigold in 1437 at Gouda. Amsterdam's own
Eglantine followed in 1496. In their early years each of these
chambers would have been under the aegis of the church, and
there would have been religious requirements for membership—contributions, attendance at mass and at requiem
masses for guild brothers. In the course of the sixteenth century these chambers were partly, some entirely, secularized.

All of this is nicely evident in the excellent broad view of the
chambers provided by Brueghel's "The Fair at Hoboken" (fig. 2,
page 36). Here we see guildsmen performing two plays in the
top right-hand corner. The tavern in front of the stage on the

right is the meeting place of one of the chambers, as we see from the presence by the door of the characteristic diamond-shaped sign board which would contain the emblem and the motto of the chamber. (The Eglantine's board, for example, can be seen in Jan Steen's "Rederijkers at the Window." It consisted of a flowering eglantine with the motto above: "Flourishing in Love."[18]) The religious procession, bearing its saints and winding its way into the church, is probably at least partly composed of chamber guildsmen, since we know that they did participate in such processions and that they did have patron saints (until the Reformation[19]). We see crossbows in the procession — and the archery contest in the foreground — because the secularized chambers sometimes interested themselves more in archery than in poetry.

In the foreground on the right we see another tavern with another chamber in residence. This chamber is flying its banner, emblazoned with "This is the guild of Hoboken." The chambers were, in fact, so nearly associated with the taverns which often provided their meeting places and much of their inspiration, and were so nearly associated with the kind of behavior that Brueghel depicts, that *rederijkers, kannekijkers* (rhetoricians, flagonseers) was a frequent taunt.[20]

However given to drink and song the guildsmen may have been, their self-proclaimed purpose was not less than the moral betterment and instruction of themselves and their townsmen. From their earliest beginnings their art was frankly religious, didactic, and often heavily allegorical. In Amsterdam, for example, there was played at the White Lavender *The Mirror of the Plague*, the sense of which was that the plague was God's instrument for the chastisement of the wicked. Listed in the *dramatis personae* are: Good Instruction, Good Nature, Scriptural Comfort, the Heart Full of Fear, Magdalene, Wrong Opinion, and other worthies. Many of the chambers met in Vlaardingen in 1616 for a competition, and there Amsterdam's Eglantine produced an allegorical drama with such characters as Time, Truth, Mars, Unrest, Discord, the Land of Batavia, and Satan. Not to be outdone, the Sunflower chamber from Ketel produced a play wherein Tyranny, Deceit, Deep-rooted Wisdom, Common Weal, Upright Instruction, and Fame all trod upon the boards. Such were not the only kinds of plays the chambers produced, but to search W. M. H. Hummelen's exhaustive listing of the hundreds of rhetoricians' plays which were printed and/or performed between 1500 and 1620 [21] is to become convinced that allegorical and biblical plays were much more the rule than the exception throughout this period.

The rhetoricians so prized their allegorical dramas, in fact, that these plays became the central feature of the many-faceted competitions, or *landjeuweelen* (literally, regional jewels or prizes). Generally, all the chambers entered in a given competition produced plays in response to a certain question. In Ghent, in 1539, the question was "What is the greatest consolation for the dying man?"[22] But the most famous *landjeuweel* of them all was that held in Antwerp in 1561, where the question was "What, above all else, moves a man to gain knowledge?" We are fortunate to have a brief account of Antwerp's *landjeuweel* written by a visiting Englishman:

> This Juell that is now to be wone, ys to be gotten by playing; and that company that can make the best answer in ther plays to the questyone that is propounded, shalle wyn the juell or pryse: weche questyone ys. — "Whatt thinge doth most cause the sprette of man to be desyrus of conying?" — So that thys ys the prynsypal pryse. Notwithstandyng, there are many other pryses to be wone.[23]

Many other prizes indeed. Prizes could be awarded for the best verse, the best pronunciation, the best banner, the best singing, the best drumming — even for the earliest arrival.[24] These competitions, by the way, give us a good idea of the literary tastes of a broad range of the population of the Netherlands at this time, for these competitions were immensely popular. There were, for example, some 1,893 rhetoricians in attendance at the Antwerp *landjeuweel* representing many chambers, and goodly amounts of gold were offered as prizes; indeed, as another English visitor wrote, "Here is nothing in this town to do, because they are still triumphing and drynking, which of the towns shall wynne the Land Jewell; wherein hath been spent above 100,000£."[25] (To put this amount of money in perspective, we might recall that at this time the entire yearly expenditure of the English crown, *in a time of war*, was about 500,000£.[26])

The Vernacular, Dialects, and Bredero's Realism

The facts that the most extravagant *landjeuweel* the rhetoricians were ever to know was held in Antwerp and that Ghent's *landjeuweel* of 1539 was not far out-glittered are important to our understanding of *The Spanish Brabanter*; for what is now the northern part of Belgium, what was then known as Brabant, was the cultural center of the Dutch-speaking world until late in the sixteenth century. Their chambers, their poets, their painters were preeminent; their churches grander; their cities — Antwerp, Ghent, Brussels — more resplendent by far than anything the north had to offer; even the Antwerp dialect, now considered endearingly quaint, was the prestige dialect of the time, the dialect of Amsterdam being considered boorish in comparison.

It is hardly surprising, then, that we should find a measure of condescension in the lordly Brabanters' attitude toward the Hollanders in the north. If the Hollanders' dialects were considered inferior, plodding, limited, incapable of treating high subjects in an elevated tone, the northerners themselves were thought to be lacking in the social graces. In one of the allegorical plays produced during the 1561 Antwerp *landjeuweel* Dame Idleness is attempting a courtly gait. " 'Am I doing it well?' she inquires from Dame Waywardness, who answers with a sneer, 'Yes, you walk like a Holland wench.' "[27]

By the time of Bredero's induction into the Eglantine, however, things were changing. In the first place, the southerners' cultural hegemony was a thing of the past. Beginning in 1585 with the flight of the Protestants from the rigors of imposed Catholicism in the Spanish-held south (of which more below), with the flight, that is to say, of a fair percentage of the skilled craftsmen, the merchants, and the brightest wits from Brabant, the south was not only crippled, but the north was correspondingly strengthened, for most of these refugees went north, and especially to Amsterdam. So many went to

Amsterdam, in fact, that they tried to retain their separate cultural identity in their adopted city. They even established their own chambers of rhetoric, the most outstanding example being the White Lavender, of which Vondel, a refugee himself, was a member. But once in the north, as A. J. Barnouw writes,

> . . . the smart show-loving Brabander was now liv-
> ing, a needy refugee, among the wealthy boors and
> wenches of Holland, whom he used to despise. The
> Amsterdam people had acquired self-confidence
> with their money and their new-won freedom [from
> the Spaniards] and felt instinctively an implied
> criticism of their own manners and customs in the
> different manners and customs of their guests. In
> self-defense, or self-justification, they repaid the
> traditional derision of the past with the same coin.[28]

Other changes were afoot as well. As early as 1550 an attempt was made to standardize Dutch orthography, and at about this same time one Simon Stevin dared to write to a learned audience in Dutch, rather than in Latin, and dared to claim that Dutch was a fit vehicle for scientific discourse.[29] Then in 1584 three of the Eglantine's most illustrious intellectuals, Roemer Visscher, Hendrick Spieghel, and Dirk Cornheert, collaborated on a volume entitled *Dialogue*, which was yet another document in praise of the Dutch language — yet another document, then, in the Dutch version of the Renaissance's elevation of the vernacular tongues. It was in this spirit too that the Leyden classicist, Daniel Heinsius, came to write poetry in Dutch rather than in Latin — Daniel Heinsius, translator of Virgil, Seneca, and Aristotle, author of volumes of highly regarded Latin poetry. That such a man should choose to write his *Emblems of Love* (1605) in Dutch was a clear sign of the new respectability of the language and a major event in the history of Dutch letters.[30]

For some the movement went beyond the championing of Dutch to the championing of specific dialects of Dutch. The *Dialogue*, for example, did not simply recommend the use of Dutch; it also urged Dutch men of letters to rid their language of "impurities" — incursions of foreign vocabulary and other extravagances which were thought to be particularly dense in the then reigning dialect of Brabant. The *Dialogue* was in effect an argument in favor of the Amsterdam dialect, which, if the reformers could manage to purge it of the southern taint, would become "pure" and "plain" and good.

It was in this milieu, then, that Bredero came more and more to rely upon—indeed, to revel in—the Amsterdam dialect; and thus it was that, when he came to write the introduction to his adaptation of Terence's *The Eunuch* to an Amsterdam setting (*The Little Moor*, 1615), he could take delight in twitting "the most highly honored masters of the far-famed Latin language," with his presumption as a "simple Amsterdammer" in forcing their beloved Terence to "prattle and babble" not only Dutch, but Amsterdams, a dialect "despised by all the neighboring cities."[31]

At the time of Bredero's entrance into the Eglantine, its members were fairly well united in and buoyed up by the increasing prestige of their Dutch language; but despite their "flourishing in love" motto, there was anything but agreement on the matter of the acceptability of the Amsterdam dialect in literary works. There were other causes of dissent as well, for at this same time such prominent members as P. C. Hooft, Samuel Coster, and Bredero began to question not only the worth of the "adulterated" southern dialect, but also much else that was near to the heart of the traditions of the chambers. They began to question the worth of the transparent allegories, began to mock the lack of verisimilitude, began to substitute rural swains for Dame Wisdom Through Proper Education, Amsterdammers for Mars and Bacchus. When, for example, P. C. Hooft wanted to comment on the political situation of the Netherlands in 1613, he did not invent such characters as Tyranny, or even Right Government; he wrote a historical drama, based on the medieval history of his own *Muiderslot* castle.[32]

Bredero also relied increasingly on local subjects as his art developed. His first play, *Rodderick and Alphonsus* (1611), was a tragedy based on an episode from one of the Amadis of Gaul romances which had been so popular in translation throughout the sixteenth century. In this first play there are two comic servants, in whose brief parts we recognize the local dialects and local color for which Bredero is so well remembered. In 1612 came *Griane*, again based on one of the Amadis stories, but this time much richer in realistic detail and comic business, with its scenes at court set off by the extended antics of a peasant farmer and his wife. Then Bredero seemed to recognize wherein his special genius lay: beginning in 1612 he wrote a series of farces, *The Farce of the Miller* (1612), *The Farce of the Cow* (1612), and *The Farce of Simon without Sweetness* (1612 or 1613), all filled to bursting with social satire and local subjects and local dialect (except where southern speech is introduced to be laughed at).

In *Lucelle* (1613) Bredero returned to romance, but, again, the play is more remembered for the antics of its minor figures than it is for the perils of its heroine. Finally came Bredero's masterpieces, *The Little Moor* (1615) and *The Spanish Brabanter* (1617) — both full of sparked language and realistic detail.

We can be sure that Bredero was helped along the road to his natural style by his appreciation of the French and English players who toured the Netherlands in the early seventeenth century. In fact, Bredero makes an explicit comparison of the foreign players — their easeful singing, their "lusty dancing," their spirited delivery of their lines — and the rhetoricians, who act and speak so "woodenly" what they have so evidently learned by rote.[33] These foreign companies were to provide more and more competition for the relatively hidebound chambers, and the broadening lessons implicit in their plays and performance techniques could hardly have escaped Bredero; indeed, some have argued that his *Griane* is in a small way specifically indebted to *The Winter's Tale*, which was one of the plays performed by an English touring company in Amsterdam in 1612.

The Eglantine could accept innovation; the Eglantine did, after all, produce the plays of Bredero very successfully, something the more conservative refugee chambers probably would not have done. Eventually, however, the rift within the Eglantine widened to the point that Samuel Coster decided that in order to accomplish his goals nothing else would suffice but the founding of a new chamber. This chamber was not to be a chamber at all, but rather a Dutch Academy. Coster wanted to take the didacticism of the traditional chambers to new heights; he wanted nothing less than an institution where not only the arts, "but the sciences too would bring their industry to bear, to edify the citizenry for love's sake and to enlighten it with the torch of the Dutch language."[34]

In 1617 Coster did found his academy, and he took Bredero and Hooft with him. Until the strict Calvinists decided that its teaching was subversive, Coster's Academy taught mathematics "to an incredible number of people," as well as Hebrew and other subjects[35] — and all of this teaching was in substantial measure paid for by the production of plays in the Academy's new wooden theater. Bredero's *The Spanish Brabanter* was one of the Academy's first productions, and Coster spoke warmly of the degree to which performances of Bredero's plays enriched the Academy's coffers.[36] Sadly, Bredero did not live to see much of this success. He completed the *Brabanter* in April of 1617. He died but sixteen months later, August, 1618, at the age of thirty-three.

The Broader Historical and Social Context

The succession of Philip the Bold to the counties of Flanders and Artois in 1384 was at once the beginning of Burgundian rule and centralization of government for the disparate peoples and towns of the Netherlands. Philip's grandson, Philip the Good, managed the major work of consolidation, adding (by inheritance, compulsion, or purchase) Namur in 1427, Holland, Zeeland, Friesland, and Hainault in 1428, Brabant and Limburg in 1430, Luxemburg in 1443, and Utrecht in 1456. For his son, Charles the Bold, it remained only to gain control of Liége (1468) and Gelderland (1473).

By the time all of this passed into the hands of Mary of Burgundy (1477), however, the Burgundians had suffered a series of important defeats, and it was probably only by marrying Maximilian of Austria of the House of Hapsburg that Mary managed to keep her inheritance together. As it was, when their grandson, Charles V, was elected emperor in 1520, Utrecht, Gelderland, and Liége had been lost to the empire, and by the time that Charles, weary of the affairs of state, abdicated in favor of his son, Philip II (1555), the shocks of rebellion and religious dissent were clearly resounding. These stirrings, taken together with Philip's uncompromising nature and the fact that Netherlanders considered him an entire foreigner (as opposed to Charles V, who had been raised in the Netherlands and who had been fairly popular), made for an altogether volatile situation. By 1564 Philip was determined to enforce religious orthodoxy among his recalcitrant Netherlanders — who were themselves ever harder put to distinguish between the religious intent of the Inquisition and simple foreign persecution.

The consequent centerless rebellion was first given direction by the Count of Brederode, who bound a group of powerful men together by oath to resist foreign persecution and to drive the Inquisition from the land. In 1566 this group presented a petition of grievances to the Spanish regent, Margaret. When the petition was scorned by one courtier as coming from beggars (*gueux*), the taunt was taken up as the party name. So it was that the furious iconoclasts of that same year were known as *geuzen*, as were the Protestant pirates who preyed upon Spanish shipping, and who eventually joined with the newly Protestantized William of Orange to combat the Spaniards openly.

Why should Spain expend such energy to hold what was essentially a marshy delta? Many reasons, but mainly: there were thriving cities in the Netherlands, cities important for weaving, fishing, manufacturing, and shipping; further, the Netherlands were ideally situated for trade, with grain coming down the Rhine, many harbors, and a location that mediated between the Baltic, England, and the Mediterranean; and the Netherlands were a strategically important buffer between Germany, England, and France.

Bredero set *The Spanish Brabanter* in the midst of this struggle, at some time shortly before Amsterdam declared itself for William of Orange and the Protestants in 1578, shortly before the formal secession of the United Provinces from the sovereignty of the Spanish king (1581). But in 1617, as Bredero was writing the play, Amsterdam and the rest of the United Provinces were entering upon their golden age. A twelve-year truce in the long war with Spain had been signed in 1609, and the ensuing period of relative peace was to enable the regents of the great trading cities of the province of Holland to open fully the floodgates of trade. Amsterdam was booming. The East India Company declared a dividend of 125% in 1610, 87% in 1612, 62% in 1618.[37] There were so many great carriages in Amsterdam that one-way traffic regulations had to be instituted.[38] The Exchange Bank, shortly to become Europe's most stable financial institution, was founded in 1609, the Lending Bank following in 1614. The new bourse, which Bredero's foppish Jerolimo affects to know so well, was begun in 1608. At the same time, Dutch shipping was coming to dominate Europe: Dutch ships were the most economical (not only were they exceptionally commodious but also their extensive use of pulleys, and their consequent ease of rigging, allowed many fewer sailors per ship); Dutch warehouses were the most numerous; Dutch interest rates were the lowest — sometimes half the English rate.[39]

Added to all these blessings was the rapid decline of Amsterdam's great rival, Antwerp. In 1585 the Spaniards captured Antwerp, and soon their depredations within were matched by a ruthless blockade by Protestant pirates without. The inevitable loss of shipping and trade was largely Amsterdam's gain. Just as great a blow to Antwerp was the Spaniards' decision to send Antwerp's Jews[40] and Protestants into exile. Many of these exiles, along with other Protestants fleeing the Spanish-held provinces of Brabant and Flanders, were merchants and craftsmen, and many of these, as we have seen, with some of their capital and all of their skills, found their way to Amsterdam.

They were not alone. German Jews also came, as did great numbers of rural laborers of all descriptions who moved into the city for the dike works, building construction, and the shipyards.[41] Between 1580 and 1604, for example, Amsterdam granted citizenship to 1,083 men to be engaged in shipbuilding and shipping alone.[42] And so the city grew. In 1612 the population of the city was 50,000; by 1622 it was 100,000; and this number was to be doubled again by 1660.[43]

Troubles came as well as growth. Indeed, there now broke upon the land a dispute so divisive as to threaten the gentle bonds which held the provinces together, and this just at a time when the fragile union had gained a brief twelve-year respite from a war with a formidable and determined foe. In an age which took its religion very seriously, it is not surprising that these troubles should bear the hazy stamp of religious controversy. In the first years of the seventeenth century a Leyden professor, Jacobus Arminius, began to teach that man was not strictly preordained to certain ends, that man was not elected by God to swell the ranks of the saved or determined previous to his sinning to suffer the fires of hell eternally, that the choices of a man's will were real choices. The strict Calvinists were alarmed. As the official church, they began to exercise their powers to prevent Arminius's students from gaining pulpits from which to spread their demeanings of the grandeur of God. In 1609 the followers of Arminius countered by presenting a petition to the governing body of the United Provinces, the States General, wherein they outlined their views and begged that they might be free to preach in accord with their beliefs. Since this petition was known as the Remonstrance, the petitioners, and subsequently all moderate Calvinists, came to be known as Remonstrants. Arminius's opponents quickly filed their Counter-remonstrance, and so they, and subsequently all strict Calvinists, came to be known as Counter-remonstrants.

Now the ripples from pebbles dropped in pools diminish in force as they leave the center, but this was an age already in preparation for the Thirty Years' War, an age which rejoiced to divide father from son, neighbor from neighbor, on either side of boundaries much more subtly drawn than the broad line of predestination. And so the dispute widened. At the insistence of the Netherlands' most influential statesman, Johann van Oldenbarnevelt, the States General sided with the minority, ruling that the Counter-remonstrants must allow the Remonstrant preachers the freedom to preach. Eventually (1614), the States General acted to suppress the public expression of extremes of doctrine, their ban reading in part as follows:

> that God the Lord created any man unto damnation,
> (or on the contrary:) that man of his own natural
> powers or deeds can achieve salvation; both

tend . . . to God's dishonour, and to great slandering
of our Christian Reformation, and conflict . . . with
our considered intention.[44]

Understandably, such pronouncements were seen by the
Counter-remonstrants as ungodly interference by the state in
matters divine. When the government went from pronouncements to the much more difficult business of en-
forcement—of bridling this recalcitrant preacher and
that—riots were the frequent result. The situation was seen by
many as paralleling the long years of religious persecution
under the Spaniards. On the other side, the Remonstrants,
along with such allies for the moment as the Catholics, the
Baptists, and the free-thinkers, were concerned lest a triumph
of the Counter-remonstrants here might make the way clear
for ever-stricter Calvinist impositions upon the flow of public
life. The dispute called into question the balance between
church and state.

Once the controversy had attained such proportions,
everyone had to be on one side or the other. This choosing up
of sides made strange bedfellows. In Amsterdam, for example,
van Oldenbarnevelt was the leader of the peace-with-Spain
party and the main force behind the government's actions
favorable to the Remonstrants. Aligned against him, then,
were not only those who opposed him for reasons of religion,
but also those who opposed the truce with Spain: the Brabant
and Flemish refugees wanted to pursue the war in order to win
back control of their southern homeland; the strict Calvinists,
the Counter-remonstrants, wanted to pursue the war with the
Spanish Whore of Babylon; others saw the war as an opportunity to gain control of the immensely profitable Spanish-held
lands in the New World; some feared that the truce would
limit their trade in the West Indies; others simply wanted to
continue the comfortable business of privateering on the high
seas.[45] To topple van Oldenbarnevelt in his dealings with the
church would be to topple him in his opposition to the war
with Spain.

With all of these interests in the balance Amsterdam's
regents finally placed the city officially on the side of the
Counter-remonstrants. In opposition to the city's official posi-

tion were Amsterdam's Remonstrants, supporters of state over church, supporters of van Oldenbarnevelt, Catholics, and moderates of all persuasions — and all those who believed, with Cornelis Hooft, that war should not be fought for religion's sake, let alone for the sake of profit. Generally, the city's literary intellectuals — P. C. Hooft, Coster, Vondel, Visscher (a Catholic), and the rest — opposed the strict Calvinists. Bredero, with his insistence on free will, his joy in life, his self-proclaimed willingness to speak frankly of matters anatomical and spiritual, with his antipathy for foreigners, his aversion to government for profit alone, and with the official Calvinist opposition to his plays — with all of this, Bredero was very much in sympathy with his fellow intellectuals.

But even such controversy could not quell his city's phenomenal expansion. The city grew despite the religious fulminations, despite the beheading of van Oldenbarnevelt in 1619, despite the public awareness of the imminence of the resumption of the war with Spain. Perhaps the best index to the mood of Amsterdam in these times was the huge land-reclamation project that was to provide the space for, and define the crescent shape of, Amsterdam until well into the nineteenth century. Exciting times. It is Amsterdam's great good fortune that these times can be so vividly brought to mind today: the buildings remain; the canals remain; the paintings of Rembrandt, Jan Steen, Jan Vermeer, Adriaen van Ostade, Pieter de Hooch remain; and there are the plays of Bredero.

The Play

The play is really a linking together of several fairly distinct sets of characters along a loosely woven plot line. Robbeknol, a rascally beggar-boy, and Jerolimo, a Brabanter who affects lordly Spanish airs, are the main characters. They meet early in the first act, whereupon Robbeknol is enlisted as Jerolimo's servant. Soon Jerolimo seeks to win the hearts of two trollops, but the objects of his dual affections spurn him once they realize his poverty. Robbeknol later wins the good will of three poor spinsters by reading to them from the Bible. Finally Jerolimo

must confront his two most persistent creditors, Geeraart Pennypinch and Beatrice, an aging bawd and renter of household
furnishings. Robbeknol and Jerolimo manage to put the two
off, whereupon Jerolimo immediately absconds, pausing only
to urge Robbeknol to be ever gentlemanly in all his dealings.
For the rest, and all along the way, we meet Amsterdammers,
born and adopted, and we listen to their talk and look in upon
their lives.

This sprawling play is based on a Spanish picaresque novel,
Vida de Lazarillo de Tormes, y sus fortunas y Adversidades
(1554, author uncertain). Bredero would have known the work
in Dutch translation as *De Ghenuechlijke ende cluchtighe
Historie van Lazarus van Tormes wt Spaingen*, in any one of
several editions (1579, 1580, 1581, 1609).[46] The number of editions indicates that Lazarus was as popular in the Netherlands
as elsewhere, but, given the feelings of the Dutch toward
Spain, I think that the extended title of the 1609 edition gives
us a special reason for the book's popularity in the
Netherlands: *The Pleasant and Farcical Story of Lazarus of
Tormes of Spain. In the Which, among other things, you may
see and come to know the Manners, Conditions, Customs, and
Roguishness of the Spaniards.*

Most of the business between Robbeknol and Jerolimo
comes fairly directly from the *Lazarus*, the main exceptions being their arguments about culture and dialect, which Bredero
supplies, along with all that is necessary to move the action
from Spain to Amsterdam. Bredero also makes Jerolimo more
prominent than his counterpart in the *Lazarus*, who there was
merely one of the masters with whom the scamp, Lazarus, had
to contend. Bredero includes all of the details of the scamp's
early life, which constitute a major part of the *Lazarus*, in the
form of a capsule autobiography which Robbeknol delivers to
Jerolimo early in act I. Almost all of the rest of the play is
either Bredero's invention or much broader adaptation.[47]

In reading the play,[48] one is soon aware that *The Spanish
Brabanter* is devoted much more to depiction of characters and
talk than to action. It is a series of set pieces, connected
thematically and by the simple forces of juxtaposition and contrast. Those who will mourn the weakness of the narrative
thread must seek consolation in the uninhibitedly vivid glimp-

ses of a seventeenth-century city that the play provides. Comparisons with the Dutch painters of the day are so irresistible that almost every account of Bredero or the *Brabanter* makes some reference to Bredero's training as a painter. The manner of that training is perhaps evident in Bredero's apology for what some evidently considered the "shameful indecencies" of the play:

> . . . we were necessitated by our choice of subject to present two women of the street in conversation. After considering the problem, we could think of nothing better than to let them speak according to their natural bent. It is reasonable and believable that they would be little interested in careful and insightful searchings of the scriptures; that they would concern themselves rather more with things of the flesh.[49]

So we are given Pale An and Tryn with all their felicitous indelicacies intact — along with all the rest of Bredero's incidental details. We can easily imagine Frans Hals and Jan Steen nodding approval. But to say that Bredero is concerned with realistic detail is not to say that his art is the verbal equivalent of *trompe-l'oeil*. Bredero would have agreed with Sir Thomas Browne, who wrote, "The world was made to be inhabited by beasts, but studied and contemplated by man."[50] Of course, this is an expression of the old notion that the world is a Book of Nature, which upon close reading will yield the same kind of allegorical significance as God's other book, the Bible. But what has happened since Augustine (see section II of *On Christian Doctrine*) is a vast expansion of the "things" that can or *should* be regarded as "signs" pregnant with spiritual significance. Browne can be interested in the "theological allusions" of the rainbow not only insofar as it is a figure for God's covenant with man. With Browne we must also

> consider that the colours are made by refraction of light, and the shadows that limit the light; that the Center of the Sun, the Rain-bow, and the eye of the Beholder must be in one right line; that the spec-

tator must be between the Sun and the Rain-bow; that
sometimes three appear, sometimes one reversed.[51]

This same kind of emblematic attention to detail the Dutch
painters devoted to their canvasses,[52] and Bredero to Amsterdam. If we are to hear how Pale An came to be a member of the
"great guild" (730), if we are to hear of Beatrice's greener days,
and lots of good seventeenth-century gossip besides, we can be
certain that, as Bredero assures us in his introductory poem,
"Instruction's here with pleasure all knit up. . . . Vice, like
sickness, must be known Before its cure" (4–8).

In the traditional rhetoricians' plays these lessons would
have been conveyed by such figures as Dame Avarice. Bredero
gives us instead a collector of hair, mussel shells, old fish,
urine, and snot balls—Geeraart Pennypinch. For Official Cor-
ruption, we get a sheriff willing to take his wage in women's
flesh; for Lust Gone to Seed, we get Beatrice; and so forth.
Bredero has not given up allegory; he has added verisimilitude
to allegory, as did Chaucer in our own tradition. But part of the
instruction Bredero promises us is more subtle than the simple
presentation of negative *exempla*; it has to do with Bredero's
whole perception of the temper of his time. For however
fascinated we may be by the vitality of Amsterdam in its
golden age, that vitality had a price, a price of which contemporary observers were keenly aware. Fynes Moryson, for example, noted that there were few churches in Amsterdam in 1617,

> Yet were these Churches seldome full, for very
> many Sectaryes, and more marchants proeferring
> gayne to the duties of Religion, seldome came to
> Church, so . . . I often observed at tymes of divine
> service, much more people in the markett place
> then in the Church.[53]

Bredero was so far of the same opinion that he depicts
Amsterdam as a diseased society. He has Floris Harmensz
enter carrying coffin scaffolding, for, as we soon learn, the play
is set in a time of plague:[54]

> With the grave digger, every night I go into the pit
> With twenty dead. . . .
> For though you had every healing herb in
>   Amsterdam,
> You're mortal still. Cork your arse, but still your
>   soul will fly.   (317-21)

The plague afflicts the body; the city's lack of concern for things spiritual afflicts its soul. To adopt the language of modern historians, such as Albert Hyma, Bredero believed that capitalism was affecting Protestantism. Hyma documents a fascinating change, for example, in official attitudes toward money lenders, a change which Bredero would have regarded as a case in point. In 1574, it seems, a provincial synod convoked at Dordrecht decided that bankers should not be allowed to partake of communion:

> No, for he has been allowed by the magistrates to
> operate his bank only because of the hardness and
> evil of men's hearts, and not because of God's will
> [God being still firmly opposed to the exaction of
> usury]. Hundreds of persons would be scandalized
> by the admittance of such a person to the commun-
> ion service.[55]

A 1627 decision by four members of the theological faculty at Leyden was in substantial agreement. A certain "Lombard" (that is, a money lender), though he had reduced his rates to sixteen percent, should still not be allowed to receive communion. Even the wives of bankers and Lombards were to be denied communion, according to the decisions of the theological faculties at Utrecht and Leyden. Hyma supplies many other examples of like kind, but, by 1658, the States General of Holland declared that "henceforth no church had the right to deprive any banker of participation in the communion service because he was a banker. In due course the other provinces followed suit."[56] This is exactly the kind of erosion of spiritual values by economic pressure that Bredero deplores in *The Spanish Brabanter*.

This disease of the spirit is so widespread that some symptom is apparent in almost everyone the play puts on stage. Where there is love, it is a commodity for sale, cash in advance, as Pale An assures us (599). The notary works on the same clear-cut basis. The sheriff has his price. The question of whether the hangman's is a desirable profession is decided by the rate of pay: "It's an honest office," says Tryn Snaps, "Oh, and it's profitable." "Well," says Els Kals, full of wonderment that anyone with wits would neglect such an opportunity, "If there's so much to gain, I wonder that men of standing don't apply" (1298–1303).

Even while we delight to see Amsterdam boys at their marble games, Bredero forces us to realize that in Kontant and Joosie we are seeing Amsterdam's next generation in training: for these boys, marbles are merchandise—"Marbles! Who wants marbles! Six for a dime!" (454)—merchandise to be bought, sold, won, or fought for. Their attitude toward their toys is fundamentally the same as Otie Dickmuyl's attitude toward the paintings (by Dürer, Holbein, van Heeskerk) he deals in—"if I can make the sale, I'll win a good amount" (2055). Merchandise, not art. Given that Bredero himself had chosen poetry above painting's "sweet remuneration," we can imagine how he would have scorned Otie's purely financial appreciation of art.

But this is not to say that the play is only about avarice. Avarice is only a symptom. The disease is, as Fynes Moryson implied, the substitution of material for spiritual values, either the inability or the unwillingness to see beyond the appearances of this world to the reality of the spirit in the Platonic and Christian sense. This is a play about Jerolimo, the Spanish Brabanter, and he is the character most obviously diseased. He is a poor rural Brabanter who affects precisely those lordly Spanish airs which the Dutch had so come to loathe in the courtiers Philip II had sent to rule the Netherlands. Jerolimo is a baker's son, a man without a penny who cherishes huge ruffs, combs, curls, and vaulting sleeves. He pretends to a wide knowledge of matters of trade and finance. He is a man with all the froth of learning—"Goddesses, you surpass . . . Wise Pallas, chaste Diane . . . Venus . . . The Spartan queen" (627–30). Jerolimo vaunts his Flemish poets and his Brabant dialect, interlarded as it is with half-understood, and sometimes wholly garbled, foreign phrases. All of this pretense from a *Brabanter*, one of those pretentious southerners toward whom Amsterdammers could now feel such comfortable condescension.

Geeraart Pennypinch offers us another example of the workings of the disease as he deftly turns the smallness of his faith into an economic maxim:

> . . . faith is small [like the Biblical mustard seed] —
> The greater the Monseur, the greater's our faith
> [that is, our willingness to grant credit],
> The greater's the thief, and the sooner he's gone.
> (1904–1906)

So, do not trust anything you cannot see. "To trust's to be deceived" (1904) is Geeraart's credo, and the credo of Bredero's other Amsterdammers. Instead of putting their faith in invisible (spiritual) things, they put their faith in appearances, in visible froth: they trust Jerolimo! Otie the art dealer, Balich the pewtersmith, Beatrice, Jasper the goldsmith, even Geeraart — they all rent their houses, consign their goods, rent their beds to Jerolimo with entire faith in his appearance of grandeur. As Otie says, "You see, I left him quite a lot. . . . I'd not have left so much had he not been plainly rich" (2056–61). After they are all undeceived, Geeraart thinks that he has learned a great truth: "The eye can well behold a man and know him not at all" (2223), but this is something that he should have learned about all the world. He should have learned to have as little faith in all the mussel shells, urine, and money he has saved at such expense of spirit. He and all the rest are like the old duffer in the story Floris Harmensz tells late in the first act; they are all blindly feeling their way through a dark world until they fall, all amazed, into a pile of . . . "mustard" (447).

The whole play is thus a set of variations on a theme by Jerolimo. But is the play, filling Amsterdam as it does to overflowing with the avaricious, the frivolous, the false, and the foolish, an indictment of the city? Not actually. I think that Bredero would say that though Amsterdam is surely sick, the sickness has not yet attacked the city in its fibers; that there is a cure, and that the cure is more than a simple call to individual citizens to abjure the Jerolimo within themselves. The larger cure is in part detailed in the proclamation that is read on the Dam (Amsterdam's central public square), as signed by Count Brederood: all the "vagabonds" and the "numbers of foreign poor" must leave "our fair city, on pain of public pillorying and whippings." This is necessary not only because the city's grain supply cannot support this added parasitic burden, but also because all these foreign poor seem to get their living "by robbery" and "godless gambling" (following 1149). The play is thus full of accusations against all foreigners, and not just the foreign poor. In fact, the reading of the proclamation interrupts an argument on the same subject. Harmen and Andries, foreigners (the former all the way from the Dutch province of Drente, some eighty miles away), argue that Amsterdam owes its riches and its intellectual vitality to foreign trade and foreign merchants. Jan, an Amsterdammer born, replies, rather amazingly:

> . . . say rather that with all our foreign trade,
> We've received many thorough-going rascals.
> Whatever's freighted or transported in
> Is worth far less, God help us, than its cost.
> The old simplicity whereof we often speak
> Has nearly all been throtled by this new deceit.
> Where is faith fled? Holland's trustworthiness?
>
> (1022–28)

It would seem that all the horrid foreigners play a kind of Lucifer to Amsterdam's Eden:

> Who brought the evil to overcome our virtue?
> Whenever I think on this, I'm sure
> That we've been slighted in the bargain,
> Whatever trade we have with foreigners. . . .
>
> (1035–38)

One of the consequences of this Fall, the contraction of this disease, is that Amsterdam can scarcely afford to take care of its own:

> The people here grow weary, giving so much away;
> They're weary of these rurals and these foreign jab-
>   berers —
> 'Tis they that pinch our deserving paupers,
> Who tearfully must hawk their shame for bits of last
>   week's bread.   (1164-67)

Lest we should doubt Jan's judgment, his views are soon cor-
roborated by Jut Jans, a spinster, one of Amsterdam's "deserving paupers":[57]

> But the people don't give much to the poor; now 'tis
>   dimes,
> Where once 'twas guilders. The paupers had it better
>   then.   (1325-26)

Later, when Els Kals, another of the spinsters, is trying to
think of some occupation for Robbeknol, she worries that
"outlanders" are getting all the work: " 'Twould be better if
Hollanders were hired" (1897). And, of course, we cannot
forget Jerolimo, the perfect foreigner — condescending, vain,
without substance, dishonest, a bankrupt, and a spreader of
spiritual disease. Even the fact that the play is set in the time
before the Protestants gained control of the city from the
Catholics and their hated Spanish collaborators is significant
in this context: *Bredero has set the play in a time when
Amsterdam was ruled by foreigners.*
    But the fascinating part of all this is that Harmen and An-
dries were right. Foreign trade, foreign merchants, and foreign
minds were essential to the making of Amsterdam. The city's
huge population expansion (from which Bredero's father, as a
building speculator, derived his tidy profit) was largely a result
of the influx of foreigners, the rurals, the exiled Protestants
and Jews, the merchants from foreign ports. Descartes,
Vondel, and Spinoza were numbered among Amsterdam's
foreigners; indeed, Amsterdam's cultural diversity was
something of a wonder in its day. James Howell's response
(1619) is typical:

> I believe in this street where I lodge there be well
> near as many religions as there be houses; for one
> neighbor knows not nor cares not much what
> religion the other is of, so that the number of con-
> venticles exceeds the number of churches here.[58]

That all of these newcomers contributed tremendously to
Amsterdam's prosperity and its culture is one of the com-
monplaces of Dutch historiography, but Bredero was convinced of the contrary. With all the talk of the unfair advantage
"the smugglers of foreign beers" (1210) enjoy by cheating
Amsterdam's tapmen of their rightful custom, with all his concern for the vats of foreign wines that avoid "the proper tax"
(1219), with all his conviction that unless tariffs are more
tightly enforced "the land'll be impoverished" (1221), it would
seem that Bredero is fondly remembering a time when tariffs
were high and trade and foreigners were *very* tightly restricted.
Two paragraphs from Geoffrey Cotterell's *Amsterdam*, I think,
provide us a glimpse of the workings of Bredero's mind:

> Medieval society was breaking down and the chief
> explosive factor was the change in commercial
> methods. . . . Medieval Europe had really been a
> vast network of restrictive practices. The towns
> were jealous of their own particular areas of
> business, and no foreigner or stranger could come in
> without being given a special privilege—as the
> Hanseatic League in London or the English "mer-
> chant adventurers" in Bruges. Trade had only been
> free at city fairs. At these restrictions had been
> eased, and anything could be exchanged, and credits
> could last from one fair to another. . . .
>
> But at Antwerp the conditions of a fair operated all
> the year round. A successful fair showed that self in-
> terest was best served not by the old restrictions but
> by promoting as great a volume of trade as possible,
> whoever did the trading. And they bought up the
> rights of the landowners who were exacting tolls on
> the river, not to exact tolls of their own but to let
> things flow.[59]

So Antwerp blossomed, just as Amsterdam was to blossom
when it had learned the same lesson. As most historians agree,
much of the tolerance that so amazed visitors to Amsterdam
was the result of the city fathers' awareness that tolerance was
profitable. This Bredero also recognized, but with stern cen-
sure. Bredero, however, was no simple-minded reactionary
concerned to cut welfare rolls. He was very much aware that
the poor must eat. It is directly after Jan's tough speech in support of the proclamation that we hear Jerolimo's poor, hungry
servant Robbeknol lament:

> God's flowing wounds, what hunger's in our house!
> We're both so still, as still as mice.
> We never speak a word, so harshly we're beset.
> No one knows such need until he's suffered it.
>   (1230–33)

The impish Robbeknol is one of hyperbole's lovers, but we
can hardly doubt that his hunger is real; however, the question
for Bredero was never whether or not it hurt to be hungry. The
question was, what might be the best way to alleviate that
hunger? An answer was readily available to him in the Dutch
tradition — the good, old Dutch response: work. P. C. Hooft
wrote the words that were inscribed above the gate to the
Spinhouse, the reformatory for wayward girls, a place where
wayward girls were kept *busy* at the work of spinning:

> Fear not, I venge no wrong, I force to good.
> Hard is my hand, but gentleness my mood.[60]

There were similar institutions for men, and in all such
places the authorities aimed to force the recalcitrant to labor,
so that the habit of labor might overcome the habits of sin and
idleness. Orphans were taught trades in Amsterdam or-
phanages; indeed, there were trade schools of all kinds in
Amsterdam and the Netherlands in these years. The consequent lack of beggars was yet another source of wonderment to
visitors. One such traveller wrote that he saw "some few beggars" in the shipbuilding town of Zaandaam, but none at all in
the provinces, and only a few in Amsterdam — and what few

there were were mostly foreigners. Those Netherlanders, he continued, who desired to be idle avoided Amsterdam, "where they shall have bread, but they must work for it."[61]

And so we must realize that however gruesome Robbeknol's plight, and however lovable he may appear (to us not less than to the adoring Els and Tryn), Robbeknol could escape his plight by his own efforts. Even if these labors prove insufficient to support Robbeknol and his hearty appetite, his efforts would at least make him *deserving* of charity. The alms he manages to get by his wits, though they be sometimes prodigious — "Fresh liver, ox snout, good bread, and sheep tripe, a sausage, a cow's hoof" (873–74) — can only confirm him in his aimless ways. As Jan says, "If folk will satisfy the dishonest wants of ne'er-do-wells, they'll but persist" (1157–58). Bredero, the moderate Calvinist, insists that Robbeknol does have free will, that he is not determined, that he can effect changes in his life. Like Geeraart, Beatrice, the trollops, and even Jerolimo, Robbeknol is what he is because of choices he has made — and choices others have made. Not for nothing does Bredero include five capsule autobiographies in this play: he wants us to see what purely human factors result in the making of whores, fops, beggars, and bawds. It was no angry Counter-remonstrant God that made Robbeknol the scamp he is, nor Jerolimo a fop.

But however Robbeknol came to be what he is, he is not all bad. In fact, the contrast between the unaffected, quick, and witty Robbeknol and the dissimulating, lumbering Brabanter Jerolimo must have appealed immensely to Bredero's fellow Amsterdammers. Just as he can learn to respect the generosity of his stepfather behind the blackness of the man's face, Robbeknol also manages to winnow away enough of Jerolimo's shallow grandeur to appreciate the small measure of good that remained: "He's a better master, even in his poverty, than were the others" (994–95). His other masters were cruel and selfish; this master is at least willing to share the food that Robbeknol begs.

The Spanish Brabanter, then, describes an Amsterdam ruled by Catholics, beset by foreigners and spiritual ills, a city too busy buying and selling to cherish the old virtues and Amsterdam's own beer. There are no heroes in the play. Like Jonson's *Bartholomew Fair,* it is a play whose norms are most often im-

plied by their contraries. We are asked to emulate none of
Bredero's characters — yet the thirty-three-year-old Bredero was
no misanthrope. He obviously enjoyed creating Amsterdammers and foreigners alike. Some of Bredero's characters appear
only for a marble game, and he is not at all afraid to have people tell stories about people we never see or otherwise hear of.
We hear loud, lewd complaints about a Jan who may or may
not be the Jan represented in the *dramatis personae*; we hear of
the death of these, of the marriage of those, and the folly of
others; and all of these seemingly uncontrolled references put
the whole of Amsterdam bustling before us. Surely this is
Bredero's most enduring quality, this uninhibited delight in
holding up a finely silvered mirror to the city he criticized out
of love.

The Text and the Translation

This translation is based on the excellent edition of C. F. P.
Stutterheim, *G. A. Bredero's Spaanschen Brabander* (Culemborg, 1974). Stutterheim's text is based on the "B" text (according to the designations of Unger's bibliography[62]). I have taken
the liberty of deleting the laudatory poems by other hands, and
I have supplied some stage directions [always in brackets] not
found in the original.

The play is difficult to translate, mainly because of the many
dialects Bredero allowed to strut upon his stage. Much of the
play's charm is a result of the interaction of these dialects — but
Bredero wrote in the dialects not for charm alone. Concerned
as Bredero and other members of the Academy were to "purify"
the Dutch language, Bredero must have seen these dialectical
variations as adulterations of "pure Dutch," as further evidence
of the evils of foreign influence in Amsterdam. The dialectal
variations and the interlardings of foreign phrases stand for
moral deviation.

To preserve the dialect distinctions, however, a translator
would have to be fluent in at least four dialects. There is
another, more fundamental, problem as well: we all have
various attitudes toward various dialects. We feel differently
about the Boston dialect now, for example, than we did before

the Kennedys burst upon the scene in 1960. It is difficult not to
think of gangsters when we hear girls referred to as "goils." To
hear that the windows "need washed," or that "dawn tawn" the
weather is "cloddy," would warm the hearts only of those who
are fond of Pittsburgh. Black English? Cockney? I finally decided, then, to make no attempt to preserve dialect distinctions. I
do, however, retain the often mispronounced foreign phrases
which ornament the speech especially of Jerolimo. I can only
hope that these phrases will keep before the reader's mind
Bredero's broad concern for the purity of the Dutch language.

 ˙ Bredero wrote his play in a mixture of free verse and Alexan-
drines. Generally, the latter were employed where the material
comes fairly directly from the *Lazarus*, free verse being the
form for the rest.[63] Bredero manages to turn this combination
into something conversational, quick, and lilting. My own ir-
regular, largely iambic verse is an attempt to match this un-
pretentious style.

Notes to the Introduction

1. As found in Geoffrey Cotterell, *Amsterdam, the Life of a City* (Boston, 1972), p. 104.

2. J. A. N. Knuttel, *Bredero: Poëet en Amsterdammer* (Amsterdam, 1968), pp. 13-14. One of the factors that contributed to the rise of Amsterdam was the amount of capital which was invested by just such "Hollanders of moderate or even small means" as Adriaen Cornelisz. See Violet Barbour, *Capitalism in Amsterdam in the 17th Century* (Baltimore, 1950), pp. 28-29.

3. Knuttel, *Bredero*, p. 18, makes this point. The letter is that to Karel Quina, for which see *De Werken van G. A. Bredero*, ed. J. ten Brink *et al.* (Amsterdam, 1890), 3:157-60.

4. John J. Murray, *Amsterdam in the Age of Rembrandt* (Norman, Ok., 1967), p. 137. Knuttel, *Bredero*, pp. 17-18, makes the same point, with a caution that we cannot be quite certain of Bredero's having lived here.

5. For Jan Steen's and other painters' membership in the Eglantine, and an explication of the Steen paintings as having to do with the chambers, see Albert Heppner, "The Popular Theater of the Rederijkers in the Work of Jan Steen and his Contemporaries," *Journal of the Warburg Institute*, 3 (1939-40):22-48.

6. *De Werken van Bredero*, 1:8.

7. K. Freise, *Pieter Lastman, Sein Leben und seine kunst* (Leipzig, 1911), p. 19.

8. Knuttel, *Bredero*, p. 14. Knuttel mentions, by the way, that Bredero would have known Lastman fairly well, Bredero's sister having known Lastman sufficiently to have been inspired to bring a breach of promise suit against the well-known painter.

9. Knuttel, *Bredero*, pp. 20-21, does suggest that certain surviving book illustrations might be Bredero's work.

10. In a letter, for which see *De Werken van Bredero*, 3:128.

11. J. L. Price, *Culture and Society in the Dutch Republic During the 17th Century* (London, 1974), p. 110.

12. Like Bredero's Jerolimo, Vondel's son ran off rather than face his creditors. Vondel spent his entire life's savings of 4,000 guilders in partial payment of his son's debts. For the lack of patronage in the Netherlands, see Price, *Culture and Society*, p. 87.

13. Actors were held in such low esteem that even as late as the eighteenth century they were still "disqualified as witnesses in court on the ground that they belonged to a disreputable calling," Murray, *Amsterdam*, pp. 124–25.

14. Murray, *Amsterdam*, p. 118.

15. Price, *Culture and Society*, p. 87.

16. The date is from Knuttel, *Bredero*, pp. 22–23. The usual date given for Bredero's entrance into the Eglantine is 1613, but I find Knuttel's argument for the earlier date persuasive.

17. See Robert G. Collmer, "Donne's Poetry in Dutch Letters," *Comparative Literature Studies* 2 (1965):27. Collmer provides a good brief account of the chambers.

18. Heppner, "The Popular Theatre of the Rederijkers," p. 25.

19. Collmer, "Donne's Poetry," p. 26.

20. Heppner, "The Popular Theatre of the Rederijkers," p. 26. See J. J. Mak, *De Rederijkers* (Amsterdam, 1944), p. 11, for the chambers as shooting societies.

21. *Repertorium van het Rederijkersdrama 1500–ca. 1620* (Assen, 1968), p. 252, for *The Mirror of the Plague*; p. 219, for the Eglantine's play; and p. 221, for the Sunflower's play.

22. Collmer, "Donne's Poetry," p. 29.

23. Richard Clough, as found in Collmer, "Donne's Poetry," p. 29.

24. Ibid., p. 28.

25. Ibid., p. 29.

26. *The Fontana Economic History of Europe*, ed. Carlo M. Cipola (Glasgow, 1976), 2:111.

27. A. J. Barnouw, *Vondel* (New York, 1925), p. 18.

28. Ibid.

29. See William Z. Shetter, *The Pillars of Society, Six Centuries of Civilization in the Netherlands* (The Hague, 1971), p. 99.

30. See Price, *Culture and Society*, pp. 97–98.

31. *De Werken van Bredero*, 2:12.

32. Shetter, *The Pillars of Society*, pp. 106–08.

33. *The Little Moor*, lines 1455–61, as found in *De Werken van Bredero* 2:65–66.

34. As found in Pieter Geyl, *The Netherlands in the Seventeenth Century, part one, 1609–1648* (New York, 1961), p. 69.

35. Ibid.

36. Jan ten Brink, *Gerbrand Adriaensz Bredero* (Leyden, 1858), 1:91.

37. Albert Hyma, *The Dutch in the Far East* (Ann Arbor, 1942), p. 67.

38. Cotterell, *Amsterdam*, p. 86.

39. See Barbour, *Capitalism in Amsterdam*, pp. 80–86, for a fascinating account of Dutch interest rates.

40. These Jews were descendants of the Jews who were exiled from Spain at the end of the fifteenth century. They were to live in Amster-

dam in relative peace and harmony until the arrival there of the Nazi boxcars.

41. Barbour, *Capitalism in Amsterdam*, p. 19.

42. Murray, *Amsterdam*, p. 57.

43. Ibid., p. 10.

44. As found in Geyl, *The Netherlands, 1609–1648*, p. 49.

45. See Murray, *Amsterdam*, chap. 2, for a good discussion of Amsterdam's factions.

46. See Ariane van Santen, "Lazarus van Tormes, Spaanschen Brabander," *Nieuwe Taalgids* 54 (1971):403–08, for a discussion of the various editions and the difficulty of deciding which edition Bredero might have used.

47. J. C. Vierhout, "Bredero's Spaanschen Brabander, vergeleken met den *Lazarus van Tormes*," *Noord en Zuid* 17 (1899):142–69.

48. Most previous scholarship on the *Brabanter* has devoted itself to the difficult task of making the play available to the modern reader. This translation would simply not have been possible without all the explanations, particularly about dialect elements, provided by Stutterheim, Stoett, Damsteegt, Leendertz, Muller, and all the others who people the footnotes of this volume. Ten Brink's huge *Gerbrand Adriaensz Bredero* provides a great deal of the background so useful to a reader of Bredero—the cultural milieu, the character of Amsterdammers Bredero would have known, and so forth. Ten Brink also makes useful connections between Aristotle's theory about comedy, as exemplified by Aristophanes, and Bredero's preoccupation with character depiction and social satire (3:1–5, 41).

Some scholars have directed their attention to the play's complex structure, most notably Damsteegt and Prudon in their introductions to their respective editions of the play. But there has been surprisingly little criticism which interprets the play as a whole, relating its historical context, themes, metaphors, and moral-social concerns one to the others. The analysis which follows is a revised version of an article which originally appeared as "G. A. Bredero's *Spaanschen Brabander*," *Spektator* 5 (1975–76):660–67.

49. From Bredero's "To My Obliging Readers," which prefaces the *Brabanter*.

50. *The Religio Medici*, 1:13.

51. *Enquiries into Vulgar and Common Errors*, 8:4.

52. See E. de Jongh, *Zinne-en minnebeelden in de schilderkunst van de zeventiende eeuw* (Amsterdam, 1967), for the didactic intent beneath the realistic surface of seventeenth-century Dutch art. See further Svetlana Alpers, "Realism as a comic mode," *Simiolus* 8 (1975–76):115–44, for a specific linking of Bredero to the comic-realist tradition in Dutch art.

53. *Shakespeare's Europe . . . Fynes Moryson's Itinerary*, ed. Charles Hughes (New York, 1967), p. 281. Moryson's characterization (1617) is typical of contemporary travellers' accounts. Marvell referred

simply to the "Dunghil Soul" of the Dutch. See "The Character of Holland," p. 113 of J. Reeves and M. Seymour-Smith's edition of *The Poems of Andrew Marvell* (New York, 1969).

54. This would have been timely. Amsterdam suffered a plague in 1617, the year the play was written. See H. Brugmans, *Geschiedenis van Amsterdam* (Haarlem, 1950), 2:403.

55. Albert Hyma, *Religious Factors in Early Dutch Capitalism, 1550-1650* (The Hague, 1967), p. 327.

56. Ibid.

57. The deserving paupers were the native, *working* poor. Els Kals, Jut Jans, and Tryn Snaps are all spinsters, and spinning was the work to which almost all of the female paupers were set.

58. *Epistolae Ho-Eliane* (Boston, 1908), 1:19. Paul Sellin (in a personal communication) cautions that Bredero would not have condemned *All* foreigners, that he would have remembered such eminent refugees as Vondel and Daniel Heinsius — whose poetry Bredero warmly praises in the dedication to Jacob van Dyck.

59. Cotterell, *Amsterdam*, pp. 28-29. See further Shetter, *Pillars of Society*, pp. 86-89, for an account of the roots of these attitudes.

60. As found in Barnouw, *Vondel*, p. 15. There is considerable scholarly debate as to whether this "work ethic" was a Protestant ethic (for which see Max Weber's *The Protestant Ethic and the Spirit of Capitalism*) or a continuation of the traditional Catholic attitudes toward work and idleness (M. J. Kitch, *Capitalism and the Reformation* [New York, 1967], is a good introduction to the controversy), but it was certainly a Dutch tradition.

61. As found in Murray, *Amsterdam*, p. 54.

62. J. H. W. Unger, *Bibliographie van Bredero's Werken* (Haarlem, 1884).

63. G. Kazemier, "De Compositie van Bredero's Spaanschen Brabander," *Nieuwe Taalgids* 28 (1934):5.

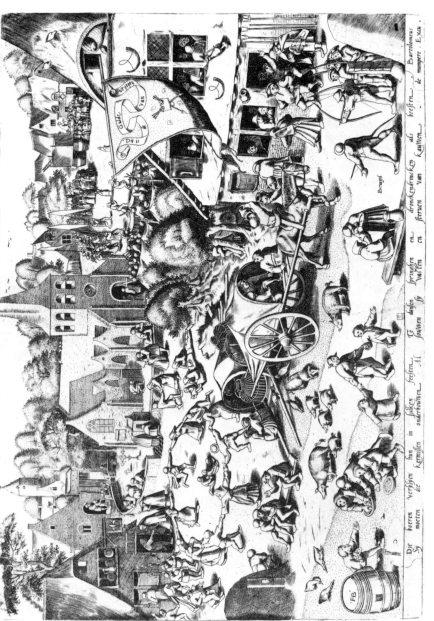

Fig. 2. Peter Brueghel the Elder. The Fair at Hoboken. Copyright

G. A. Bredero

The Spanish Brabanter

Dedication

To the noble Lord, my Lord
Jacob van Dyck,*
royal councillor and ambassador
acting in the name of and on behalf of the serene and
almighty Lord and King, Gustavus, the second of
that name, the King and heriditary ruler
of Sweden, Gotland,*
and Wenden, Grand Duke of Finland, Duke of
Estland, and West-Man-Land.*
Residing with the high and mighty Lord of the States
General of the United Netherlands.

The sky is never so steadily draped with restless burdens of
darksome clouds all pregnant with the bawling tempest, but
that even then the rage of these her heavy labors is bright lit:
she then gives forth her flickering, joyous rays of happiness. So
it is also, my lord, with the heart of man. Man cannot be
always listless, heavy-minded, however great and weighty
matters he may bear upon his back. One must sometimes seek
to free one's self from hinderances and earthly troubles. I
believe that it was to this end, and for such as are thus heavy
burdened, that enlivening, gladdening poetry was conceived.
Poetry, say I, not only rejoices and ornaments the heavens and
the earth as does the godlike sun; it also comes to penetrate the
inner-most unknowable recesses of the soul. Along the shim-
mering rays of amusement poetry speeds to the noblest and
most secret chambers of illustrious hearts,* wherever poetry,
in its wondrous way, overwhelms the excellent understanding
of the learned and the godly. As for example: can any man be so
clodlike, so murky of spirit; can any mortal hear or read
without attention, without being moved, the divine hymn *Iesu
Christo* written by the most learned Daniel Heinsius?* I do not

believe that such a mortal lives who could not be moved and yet be endowed with rational faculties. For myself, I might well say that I regard this hymn as the most exalted poetry that has ever been. I have derived more benefit from this hymn than from any other in my life, and I am convinced as well that it is also prized above all by your lordship.

Now, among other honors bestowed upon me by your lordship is that of your honoring my rustic verses with the glorious brilliance of your most noble condescension in reading and enjoying those poems. This so emboldens me, worthy lord, that I dare to dedicate my *Spanish Brabanter* to you, full well convinced that your most noble inclination will be not to disdain my little gift, but rather, with an obliging disposition, to take the same with thanks. I pray your most noble lordship that your most noble judgement will so strengthen my *Brabanter* that undaunted he might meet his enemies* (whom he does not fear).

In this faith I commend your most noble lordship to the graceful favor of your king and of the King of kings, that you might be preserved in all bliss, so well temporal as eternal. With all my heart, this is the wish of your most ready servant and friend,

G. A. Brederode.

To My Obliging Readers

If men were created with such good nature that they were quicker to aid improvement and slower to berate faults, we'd all be nearer to a divine perfection; we would see our little souls in all respects improved. But, alas, we are of a fallen nature, more careful of the mote in our neighbor's eye than of the beam in our own. Oh, palpable fault! None worse! Each man fawns upon himself and fondles his own errors, but whatever the faults of his acquaintances these he chastens with all his force. What prejudiced, blind, and forgiving judges we are in covering over our own misdeeds; what corrupt hangmen and hellish tyrants we are as regards the slips of others—we pillory them. Poor creatures that we are, we are wont to cover our own faults with an elegant mantle, as blithely as though we thereby performed God a tremendous service; not once considering that we have so much to correct and restore within ourselves that we never have to go outside ourselves to find such labor: everyone has sufficient work in his own garden. But in reality? All eyes look outward; none look inward.*

And I too wander in this common thoroughfare, describing my neighbours' waywardness — as is the custom of writers and poets. I picture forth for you, all nakedly, the infirmities of our age, the abuses of our times and of this depraved world—even the everyday indiscretions of the common man. Yet in the midst of all this, I do not forget my own weaknesses, and as I pray to the Almighty that He will come to my aid and yours, He knows that I do this not out of hate, neither to incense nor to embitter any man. I have rhymed and written only to amuse and improve.

Should it then come to pass that I, all unawares, should anger any respectable, pious, upright, and virtuous persons, I herewith earnestly beseech that they impute my error to my unwitting and my little knowledge; I beseech that they excuse my offence and return me good for ill. I would then be compelled to follow their example, and bear my enemies, detractors, and slanderers patiently. With my heart at peace, with entire good will, I could shoulder then their contumely: for just as undeserved praise can do me no good in its excess, so the vilifications of the faultfinders, the prejudiced, the angry, those who are eaten up with bad will and bias, those who will allow no thing, howsoever good, to stand undespised or unvarnished by their opinions—the detractions of such as these are equally ineffective. In contrast, the unprejudiced, the impartial are not anxious about the impertinent pronouncements of such drudges: they differentiate, they discriminate, they sift, they test, they try the worth of whatever is before them with unsullied truth as their touchstone.

Some learned Doctors (whether they bear the title with right or not), who are held in high regard by dissembling hypocrites, some of these learned Doctors have slandered our Spanish

Brabanter without ever having seen or heard him. Consequently, we have decided that we will let him see the light of day, so that he, before all the world and everyone, might answer those who, in their sanctimonious innocence, have convinced many that he is guilty of shameful indecencies.* Hereby their lies and his probity shall be revealed. Neither he nor I would disavow that there are things about him that are not above reproach, but who or what is perfect in all things? There is nothing that is blameless save God. But just as the comedies and farces of antiquity dealt with nothing else than the common foibles of man, so we write in the same fashion, according to our own limited experience, of the worldly doings of our people, not presenting matters beyond their understanding or their daily experience. That is, a smith knows his iron and his coal, the painter his paints, the shoemaker his lasts, the which is quite natural and becoming.

Now, we were necessitated by our choice of subject to present two women of the street in conversation. After considering the problem, we could think of nothing better than to let them speak according to their natural bent. It is reasonable and believable that they would be little interested in careful and insightful searchings of the scriptures, that they would concern themselves rather more with things of the flesh. They would not be inclined to make weighty pronouncements on the basis of angelic understanding. If their lecherousness is somewhat unrestrained and immodest, we are not the first to so depict them: the Greeks and the Latins cheerfully precede us. This is apparent in Aristophanes, Plautus, Terence, and a few other unabashed souls—whom nonetheless the learned in our schools give to youths for their amusement and delectation. This proceeds without question, while whatever is placed for its moment upon the stage is damned by everyone as all but a deadly sin, while everyday on the street and in their houses and elsewhere (God shield them) they hear and do worse. These and such like scabby sheep do bleat the most,* while those with warmer hearts can well allow a poet to take the godless and the deceitful somewhat to task.

I know that it is a slackness in me that I can not coddle the honorless, willful bankrupts-for-profit (those who abuse the respectable for their own ends, making upright citizens poor and sorrowful as surely as do thieves). Nor can I be as polite to them as they are to the rogues and robbers with whom they share their loot — those who are sick of the same disease. They pronounce bankruptcy one day, but are doing very well the next. I may be a man of little worth, but I am possessed of sufficient goodness of heart that I cannot tolerate such knavery, such damnable rascalry; nor can I, without complaint, suffer any to come to sorrow through no fault of their own. Now, in truth, I have not meant anyone in particular: I have thrown my cudgel, hit or miss, at a pack of a hundred. He who is hit might heed the rhyme: "The more the present pain, the more the future care."

I have been so far discreet that I have chosen another time, so that my readers will think less of making connections in the present, just as I myself was little concerned with such correspondences. I have included Brabant dialect for no other purpose than to display its haughty poverty. It has its grotesqueries as well as does our blunt Holland tongue. Brabanters can no more follow the convolutions of their erroring speech than we can. These, then, friendly readers, are the considerations which have moved me to print my Brabanter, who has been so shamefully slandered, and who will, I hope, please you as he has previously pleased some of our best and most honorable citizens. If it prove so, I will hasten to bring your honors an even more farcical, an even livelier play. I will not keep you longer. Read with pleasure and apply that which applies to you. If I'm given a friendly smile for my pains, it will be enough.

Yours, ever willing and affectionate,

G. A. Bredero.

G. A. Bredero to the Reader

If aught that's wrong you notice here,
        Learn then to shun its like.
I've not written to commend these paths;
Instruction's here with pleasure all knit up.
    If what you find displeases you,
        Man or maid, see there a lesson.
    Vice, like sickness, must be known
        Before its cure. A child,
        With his little understanding,
Will walk into the fire though it burns him,   10
        While those who know its pain
    Can see the flame's too hot for them;
        They handle fire otherwise
        And find both use and warmth.
    My prayer is that you'll find use in this,
    That this might warm your will to good.
    Now, those who judge mischief's born
        When its true nature is declared,
    When sin, as sin, is openly revealed,
        I'm sure have missed the mark.   20
    Take the preacher on his pulpit:
    When he makes known the heresy
        Of some sophist lost to honor
        Or some godless atheist —
        Does the preacher evil then?
        Is virtue thus diminished?
    Nonsense! Do all our magistrates,
    Authorities, do all wise councils
    Aid evil's progress through our land
        When they punish regicide?   30
        Or rape? or thievery?
        Or rowdyism? arson?

I believe they hardly do.
Do plagues and diseases
Enter our bodies' members
Because the doctor comes?
There's as little chance, and maybe less,
Of evil's forcing entrance to a soul;
For truly pious hearts
Resist everything but good.   40
A thing may be then great or small,
But pure is ever pure,
And evil will incline to ill.
It may be said that it's with them
As 'tis with spider foul:
It consumes what's good with ill intent;
The flower's nectar turns to venom
Within its tight black bowels.*
Many Hollanders are the same:
One play they'll slander, praise another,   50
According to their predispositions,
And not from knowledge of our art.
In such loose brains is ground
The praise or blame which men do win.
Now some I've hit unwittingly:
When these decry my words,
I cannot blame them, not at all.
For these I hope that all goes well,
In health and soul, all as they might and wish—
As well as any living man.   60
To you enlightened worthies,
Who speak kindly of my work:
You'll find here but a simple rhyme,
Without the scent of Greekish thyme
Or Roman herbs, but like the flowers*
Of Holland, it may be widely known.
What though this have no scent of thyme?
'Tis Amsterdam's own bud,
A simple Netherlandish herb,
Which gives out no more sweetness   70
Than is looked for. Then if its taste is wrong,
Combine it with those nectars

Which your widely ranging minds have sucked
Out of the best of books,
And make honey in your hive —
Where I do hardly dare to enter in,
Because, as I freely do admit,
I'm the least of all the bees.

All is changeable.*
Anno Domine, June 6, 1618

The Argument of the Play

Of the few outstanding wits to be found among the Spaniards, the author of *Lazarus de Tormes* is not the least, but is, in my judgment, rather to be regarded as one of the most important, for he surely and subtly points out and condemns the faults of his countrymen. Him we follow here in the first book [of the *Lazarus*], wherein the author depicts the pride (which seems inborn) of his paltry nobleman. But, because we have no Spaniard, because the common man would not understand [his Spanish] if we did have a Spaniard, we have changed the names, the places, and the times, and we have changed the Spaniard into a Brabanter. Brabanters do fairly resemble Spaniards after all. The matter has been divided into five acts, as is our wont.

In the first act Jerolimo tells of his coming from Brabant, his reason for coming being the difference between Amsterdam and Antwerp, between the two peoples and their customs. He tells as well of his former grandeur, and all with preposterous pride. He takes into his service a threadbare beggar boy with whom he saunters about the streets in idle display, until they finally go off to mass. Three old, dry-skin fellows then show forth, by their simple manners, speech, and coats, the true simplicity of Amsterdammers. They show us the time as well, namely the time of the plague more than forty years now past.

In the second act Jerolimo, being thoroughly brushed up, meets two light wenches at the fortifications at the mouth of the Amstel. With these he plays the perfect courtier. The wenches, more inclined to heed his money than his lovely words, desire him to conduct them to the Guardhouse.* Jerolimo, his purse as hollow as his stomach, makes many trifling and dishonest excuses, and then most respectfully takes his leave with many a bow and quaint nod. The wenches make merry as they walk, and tell the beginnings of their lewd and unholy life. In the meantime the hungry Robbeknol goes begging, in the which he is so fortunate that he is enabled to victual both his own empty belly and his poor but good-hearted master's. Well satisfied, they then go forth together to seek repose.

In the third act Robbeknol tells the story of his life and adventures. Then, his master being away, Robbeknol searches for his purse, discovers it, explores it, only to find it rich in folds but poor in pennies. Then the three old fellows declare each the faults of the others, in the midst of which the City Bell is rung. From the steps of the City Hall it is proclaimed that begging is forbidden, on pain of whippings. Measures are announced concerning the truly poor as well. All of this is praised by all but Robbeknol and others similarly circumstanced who complain of the ordinances. A brawling wife next raves and rants to distraction, but she is calmed by two spinsters, her neighbors. Robbeknol, making a virtue of necessity, approaches these women reading the seven psalms,* and thus he gets his bread. Jerolimo, having come by a bit of coin, now fancies himself the richest man alive. He sends his servant for food and drink, but Robbeknol meets a funeral procession on his way, hears a few words, and runs aghast back to the house. But this passes and he goes out upon his errand.

In the fourth act a bawd tells of her life and trade. Robbeknol, loaded with edibles, is happily met by Jerolimo, and they fall to with a will. During the meal Jerolimo tells of his ancestry and other foolish matters. They are interrupted by Geeraart Pennypinch, Jerolimo's landlord, and Beatrice, the secondhand dealer, who have come to dun. After making manifold promises [to Geeraart and Beatrice, Jerolimo persuades them to leave, and then] the poor devil runs off, a bankrupt.

In the last act the neighbors, having come to know of his departure, inform the dunners and the creditors of Jerolimo's bankruptcy, whence arises a furious commotion. The sheriff, notary, and witnesses having been fetched, the house is opened. They find within but one small cot, which, after much debate, is carried off to the City Kitchen.* The result is that all

the creditors receive equal compensation—they leave unpaid
and unsatisfied. There you have it all, as the goodwife said as
she spat her heart up out of her body.*

Dramatis Personae

Jerolimo Rodrigo . . . . . The nobleman [the Spanish Brabanter].
Robbeknol . . . . The servant.
Joosie   ⎱
Kontant ⎰ . . . . Two lads.
[Aart   ⎱
[Krelis ⎰ . . . . Two lads.]
Floris Harmensz . . . . Church beadle.
Jan Knol   ⎱
Andreis Pels ⎬ . . . . Aged fellows.
Thomas Trek ⎰
Tryn Jans ⎱
Pale An   ⎰ . . . . Two strumpets.
Tryn Snaps⎱
Els Kals   ⎬ . . . . Spinsters.
Jut Jans   ⎰
The wife of the deceased, and others with her.
Beatrice . . . . A junk dealer and bawd.
Geeraart Pennypinch . . . . The landlord.
Notary
Clerk
Two witnesses
Balich . . . . A pewtersmith.
Jasper . . . . A goldsmith.
Joost . . . . The neighbor.
Otie Dickmuyl . . . . The painter.
The sheriff and his officers

ACT I

[*A street in Amsterdam.*]

JER: This city's *magnafique*, but what a grubby folk!
In Brabant we're all quite exquisite
In dress and bearing — in the Spanish mode —
Like lesser kings, gods visible on earth.
Oh, imperial Antwerp, great and rich!
In all the sun's wide range there's nowhere else
Such abundance of slime* and comely fields,
Triumphant churches, cloisters most devout,
And stately buildings, lofty ramparts,
And overarching trees along the piers   10
And quays where flows the mightly Scheldt
Right up to Meyr Square.* How grand 'twill be to tell
My ventures to the maidens there about the bar —
Dear Betty, May, and her niece, the lovely Klaar:
She has such a motion as she trips about,
That she's adjudged the prize of Lepelstreet,*
And all the Venus district — such grace!
The castle's regent, the lusty gallánt,
Loved her past distraction.
What bodices and aprons he's given   20
To bed her. I myself was amorous:
Annette de Tourney, Janny de Geus —
Oh, lovely goods, cordial queens,
They meet the world in such stately fashion.
Ah, had I been less the banqueteer,
I'd been there less the scandalous bankrupt too.
All was well. Why seventy pair of sleeves* I had
Which my *creditéurs* demanded I return:
So all the merchandise I hired here in Amsterdam*
I gave those *creditéurs*. I feared the sheriff;   30
For I was sure they'd set him on me;
That soon enough I'd be in prison or the stocks.
I rather dwell with melodious, warbling birds,
Than in odious stinking, iron-clanking holes.
When one of these new *creditéurs* confronts me —
A quick lie, and a trifle in his hand.

I've managed now for, oh, a month or so.
So many goodly souls in Amsterdam
Trust their goods to others, like myself,
Who will abscond with all that we can get.   40
To see a man's facade (as here we read*)
Is not to gauge his heart.
But now 'tis time to play upon these blockheads:
We've each our little comedy to stage!
What else? Alas, I know no rest. No pence for me.
For if I'm rich, my wealth's invisible!

                    (*Exit Jerolimo.*) [*Enter Robbeknol.*]

ROB: While my wounds were red, bandages and all,*
I got, for grace of God, whatever I pleased.
But now, alas, I'm healthy, mended!
Now it's: "Go to work, you lazy beggar!   50
You're young and strong! Alms to you is sin.
'Twould be to rob the rightful poor."
What now? Not thievery. No, I loath it.
It's a pleasant art, but thieves are often hanged.

                    [*Enter Jerolimo.*]

A servant? I'd then have board at least,
A roof, relief for my poor empty belly —
I'll gladly serve any wealthy master.

                    [*He notices Jerolimo.*]

God's bloody bones! What tassels to his legs!
A lordly fop; he's positively gilded.
JER: Hark, lad, do you seek a master?
ROB: Indeed I do, my lord.   60
JER: Well, come with me; you'll never want again.
You've doubtless said your little prayers today,
For God has blessed you with a proper master.
ROB: My lord, I'll be to you a proper servant.
JER: Your name?
ROB: Robbeknol, at your service.
JER: Oh, you're a nice one.
Whence come you then?
ROB: From Embden, God help me.*

JER: One of Embden's potshooters!* I might have known.
ROB: Yes, yes, Amsterdammers, Brabanters — they know it all.
JER: True, true. Your parents, do they live?
    What's your family?
ROB: My father's born in Bolsward: 70
    He's a Fries.* My mother hails from Alkmaar.*
    After many wanderings and doings, they met.
    He was a miller; mother hired out bulls.*
    And though I say so, well she knew her trade.
    She could tell, just by looking at the cow,
    If it'd take. But now, alas, no more:
    Sly Piet, my revered father (I'll not mince about),
    Took a bit more flour than he ought.
JER: A common offense, quite the fashion here.
ROB: The millers, my lord, they see it otherwise: 80
    They play at give and take.* Still, he was found out,
    And flogged, and driven from the town.
    Then he joined the Spaniards in the war here.
    Don't know what he did to them — they poisoned him,
    So that he died. When my mother, Aaltie Melis, heard of
            this,
    She took me and all she had to Amsterdam
    And hired a cottage, hung "The Count of Embden"*
    As her sign and rented beds. Sailors' shirts
    And other clothes she washed on empty wharves.
    Then soon Lord Duckdalf's* groom's man she came to
            know,   90
    For look, 'twas he brought all his master's linen to be
            washed.
    An ugly black he was. She was passable.
    Not bad. (But fagh! When a woman's green
    She'd do it with the hangman, dogs, or Satan's self.)
    My mother was a widow, lusty, hot of blood,
    Who remembered all too well how sweet a bed could be.
    What was she to do? She laid the moor,
    To prove were blackamoors so supple soft as people say.
    The rogue, he filled her hard as any nail —
    In fact, he filled her with a little black.   100
    So happy was she that I began to worry.
    The moor, he brought sweet gifts of every kind —

Of sugar, wine, of game, of little birds,
And other tasties. Now a capon, then a duck,
A larded dove,* a whole-roasted snipe:*
'Twas thus he eased her in her pregnancy. "Ah," said he.
          "My love,
Do eat a bit. 'Twill do you good." I stood off and watched.
Sometimes I'd get a bit of what was there.
Soon enough I came to like him, and his visits too.
Before, I'd howled and screamed whenever he came
          near —   110
For very fear I'd shiver when I saw him come.
I'd cry, "A thunderstorm is coming up —
It's so dark there yonder!" I thought he was the Devil
Or some hobgoblin; but the more I saw of pastries, bread,
And other treats, of wine as well as food,
The more he seemed an angel, not a man.
All this went on for, oh, a year or two.
Then one day, when he was dawdling with his son,
Petting him and bussing him — for he loved him with all
          his heart —
The child saw that we were white, his father black as
          pitch.   120
He sprang to his mother, all afraid, and cried:
"Oh mama, mama! Help me, help! The Devil's there!"
He grinned and then he taunted both child and mother too:
"May the gallows stretch you, you bloody little whore's
          whelp!"
Now I was young, but that I understood.
Ah, thought I, how common 'tis that men
Do rudely blame and scold another
For those faults foulest in themselves —
While those they blame are faultless as my brother.
          But I'll be brief, my lord. The stable master   130
And the overseer observed his traffic to and fro.
They laid for him — spied and watched,
Until they'd seen him grabbing, stealing
Oats and hay, and bridles, brushes, bits, and spurs,
And blankets, bear hides, and more than I can name —
Even shoes right off the horses' hooves.
All of these he sold to smiths and waggoners at half their
          worth.

From the house he stole whatever was loose—
Copper, tin, and silver spoons, platters, cups, and plates.
If truth be told, he was a thief straight from the womb. 140
And was he asked? Oh, he knew nothing, or 'twas lost.
All this for love—all for my mother and brother.
Don't you wonder at all these fellows
Who'd steal money from their mistresses
To pay a whore for a moment's pretty play?
          Well, soon they caught me, locked me up.
What could I do, my lord? For fear, I told them all I knew:
How all he stole she sold for whatever she could get.
They let me loose when they'd heard me.
They caught my moorish stepfather then by the neck, 150
Stripped him mother-naked, lit a flitch of bacon,
And let it drip, burning, on his back.
Like an eel he writhed, but couldn't get away,
So, hard though 'twas, he bore it patiently.
My mother was forbidden converse with the moor
On pain of long imprisonment.
They mentioned other correctives too.
"Burning bacon," thought my mother, "would not please
          me:
If I've lost the ball, I'll not throw the club."*
Because of all the gossip then, and to get her bread, 160
She went in pure devotion to the old folks' hospital,
Where she served God's will to gain her board.
And there too, as well as I could, I earned my keep:
I'd run for potions to doctor or to druggist;
For salves to barbers, and on other errands for the sick.
Finally there came a cocky, withered, bastard blind man,
Who wanted me for guide. He talked my mother so
          around,
That she gave me over to the scoundrel—
Ah, master, I tell you, 'twas quite a year!
Could you but know what pains I've suffered. 170
JER: Now, Robbeknol, 'tis well now. Tut, lad, be calm,
And thank our Lord for His good grace,
For now your trials are past: with grand munificence
I'll now provide whatever you need.
But one thing saddens me: your uncouth Dutch—
Oh, the speech of Brabant's *heroïque*, stately, flawless,

So friendly, *spirité*, tender — propriety itself!*
'Tis hard to tell its virtues. If only you
Could master the quiet perfection of my speech —
Par dieu, lad! — you'd then forsake your ugly Dutch!   180
Whoever can follow us can any tongue construe.
Why, better yet — I'll make of you a Brabanter!
Our language is a rhapsody — ah, *non paréel*,
No comparison* 'twixt Brabant purity and plodding
    Dutch.

ROB: Yes, 'tis a pretty mishmash, as best you know.
There's French, some Spanish, and Italian all thrown in.
I'd say you even beat the English and the starlings* there.

JER: *Santo Jesu*, what brainless bumpkins have we here:
Crimped and poor their lives, their written style simple.

ROB: God's nails, if I could winnow out your ugly Brabant
    speech,   190
As spice mongers do their spices, why, I'd wager
Not half of what you babble would remain.
And if a Brussels court would ban that winnowed foreign
    chaff,
So everyone would have to speak according to their native
    sense,
Or what he'd heard at home — oh, what a sight —
You'd all stand naked, gaping at your homely little speech.
But no. 'Tis all so tightly mixed that not even all
Leyden's and Louvain's professors* could begin to sift it
    out.

JER: *Idiotisme* — take your acts notorial.
No hint of courtly terms? In simple Dutch?   200
Our notaries, our secretaries understand pronouncements,
And all they do is authorized with seals, grants,
    privileges —
All from the Imperial court itself! Such *elegánce!*

ROB: Could the Roman pope and all his cardinals wrench them
    from their theme?
These Brabanters all see themselves as witty authors:
Whatever they pen's as novel as a babe to's mother.

JER: When last we held the Land's Jewel Rhetorical* —
'Twas other worldly, a feast for eyeballs —
Where were Holland's scribblers then? None shown forth.

Jesu, par dio santo, what stately poets were there.   210
Item: Kastileyn, de Roovere, Gistellen, Kolyn,
and Jan Baptisten Houwaart* — masters, by the Lord above!
Fellows of *perféccion, deviné eloquencíe* —
Their every word was full of high *senténce;*
Their every breath a refrain* — more lusciously ex-
          travagant
Than East Friesian sermons, or even Lutheran.
Their *rondelets* and *ballades*, may I say, would force
Holland's peasant-poets* to hide their pens for shame.
ROB: Whatever you do, don't disregard the Flemings, master:
     Such marvels as "Palace of Love." and "Sweet Sugar
          bunches."*   220
JER: Tut, wait a bit, enough of these fusty rhetoricians,
And don't make faces. Compose your face as I do,
And 'twould be well to walk in stately, graceful manner,
          thus.
And don't wrinkle up your face — hold it set in lofty
          fashion.
Oh, *exceptionál!* Well done. *Magnafique* — how genteel!
Now, neatly clean and brush your clothes and all ac-
          coutrements:
Fetch the brush; do it all directly, won't you?
I'd give a thousand pounds to make of you a Brabanter:
I'd present you to the greatest in the land;
With your knowledge, monstrous huge, I'd promote you —
          Doctor of Law.   230
You'd be the world's marvel. You'd rise to greatness:
For I would make you king of Holland or of France.
The title of marquis or count's not worth a rag;
Captaincies and dukedoms, colonelcies — these I'd give to
          children.
To think of such slight trifles is to overprize them;
Why, I'd give away all Gelderland without a thought.
I have liberality in common with our king,
Who gave a simple captain all that India,
Which his soldiers' force had just won for him.*
Now I must go join the cloister nuns for mass.*   240
But first, I'd ask you, are you debauched?
Nothing's better for a man than sparse living.

The thrifty prosper. To eat or drink to excess is beastly.
ROB: [*aside*]: I recognize this tune. I know which toe is out of
          joint.
     I do believe that I was born on Galpert's Eve;
     Three days before the day of luck.* Lost again.
     The devil always helps me to these misers.
JER: What are you mumbling there?
ROB: Not a thing, my lord.
     Don't worry, I'm no eater. We'll manage well enough.
JER: An onion, a leek, a bit of bread, and two figs—   250
     A lordly meal.
ROB: A bit of meat, a pound or six,
     Is also not amiss. Some quarts
     Of Dantzig beer or manly Rostock's brew*—
     I could do with such for an hour or three or four.
     Any seven men would, in wisdom, do the same.
JER: Such men would squander food and waste their means—
     Sobriety's a virtue such men could never understand.
ROB: In simple Dutch: "Don't eat too much."
JER: 'Tis so healthful to eat abstemiously.
ROB: This advice should then be given to the sick.   260
JER: *Monseur*, the *temperancie* is divine!
ROB: My lord, 'tis so good that most would rather feast.
JER: What difference, then, between such swine and glut-
          tonous beasts?
ROB: The greatest drunks are the most inspired.
JER: Who then? Hank, Willy, and Wuytie? Fine lot!
ROB: 'Tis the learned men that drink the wine.
     —Not that I speak for my humble, fasting self—
     But sure, it's farmers who'll not think of sugared Rhenish
          wine.
JER: These Hollanders, *par die*, they drink like moffs, like very
          poops,*
     And they're barbarous in their cups: they scream and
          call   270
     Like the brainless fellows that they are. Brabanters are
          modest:
     Of an evening, we dine in moderation, soberly;
     We court the ladies with discourse never *vulgáire*.

We delicately do feign to hold great sway in great affairs;
The trade of India and Guinea's all our talk;
I fancy I see angel legions
When our pretty maids walk by; we've all a pleasant wit.
ROB: I'd guess we're much alike. You've been around I see.
God's sweaty blood, I've such a hunger. My jaws do lust for
    work.
My belly's of opinion that my neck's been hanged.*   280
JER: Now, let's to church, to the Brothers of Our Lady, and
    hear mass,*
Then we'll see about a fish or meat.
ROB: Oh, there's a forceful word, according to my inclinations!
Oh priesty, priesty, please be quick, so I can eat!

                [Exit Robbeknol and Jerolimo.]
(Enter two boys and Floris Harmensz, a beadle, carrying a cof-
    fin scaffold.)

AART: Grayhairs, will you play at bones with us?
I guess up, old grayhairs!

          [They throw bones at Floris.]

Oh, poor old cripple's lost his bones!*
HARM: By God, you gallows-birds! You gallows-birds!
Let me be, or else, I swear I'll beat your ears!
What a plague these whoreson, damned rascals are.   290
Should I catch you in the church, I'll truly lock you up!
KRELIS: Cripple, cripple, crooked-leg!
You are a gallows-bird; you are a gallows-bird!
HARM: Why do these hell-fired picklocks ride me so? If I catch
    you,
'Sblood, I'll bullpizzle* all that's holy in you!
You'll not soon forget! God's lights, I'll thrash you so,
That, by God's sacraments, you'll next time hold your
    tongues.
AART: Grayhair cripple, grayhair cripple — if you'd dare
We'd turn that knife and twist it in your guts.
HARM: I'll put this scaffold down and then — you damned pick-
    pockets!   300

         [They throw stones.]

KRELIS: There's for grayhairs!

HARM: Oh, catch those two!

[*They run out.*]

Catch 'em by God's will. Get 'em! Run you rascals!

How these miserable, damned, devil's own knaves do tor-
         ment me.

They vex me so, and me a cripple too. God help me.

My legs they tremble. They can't support me.

(*He sits on the scaffold.*)
[*Enter Jan Knol, Andries and Thomas.*]

JAN: Well, Floris Harmensz, who's dead? Where goes the scaf-
         fold?

HARM: Ariaan the Pint,* Dame Barber's husband — your mate
         in cups.

AND: Ariaan the Pint's dead? Dead? Dead? 'Tis a wonder:

Trust me, there wasn't a healthier man in town,

Nor a stronger, both in flesh and limb.   310

JAN: Too bad he was a stiff-necked, thickheaded foreigner.

THOM: Well, let be the dead; don't speak ill of those who've
         gone.

HARM: Uncle Thomas, there you're right — your great friend he
         was.

JAN: Was he long a'bed? What sickness got him?

HARM: They say it was God's gift.*

JAN: Then do you dare go in?

HARM: Oh, won't I dare? I not go in? Nice, yes.

With the grave digger, every night I go into the pit

With twenty dead. I think: If my name's there on God's
         roll,

There goes my head. And all our names are on that roll;*

For though you had every healing herb in Amsterdam,* 320

You're mortal still. Cork your arse, but still your soul will
         fly.

The people run for fear; but go as far as Texel,*

Death still comes to all, yes, though you build a wall about
         yourself.

Death spares neither small nor great — no shield 'gainst
         death.

Do good while yet you can, and live as you would die.*
'Tis an art to live when death is near, as Nabuur said—
What said Malegys when the plague began? "I'll save me!"
All Dr. Schol his drugs he bought and laid 'em in a chest.
But 'fore he knew it, 'twas he was laid to rest.
His friends and kin, they cried 'til eyes came near to
      floating out   330
(But after five or six or so had died, they soon forgot).
     Now all's well, but at the first they worried
      mightily
Whether he might decently give up the ghost:
For look, his nose was hooked down over his mouth,
So his ghost no sooner left him than, post quick, 'twas
      back in's nose,
Over and over, so that his soul could not depart him.
Now I'll tell how old Gys he finally came to die:
He left his back door open, do you see,
And thereby, invisibly, his ghost did fly.
        Poor Gys, he was ashamed: 340
For though he was a laborer, he wanted
To appear a merchant, though he was the poorest noodle.
What are these boasters but the slaves of whims?
For though they may be rich, they spend themselves to
     poverty.
Still, you I prize, Jan Knol; you'll never buy land.
Why should you save for mother or brother?
JAN: Old grayhairs, that's enough from you. You're quite a
    talker.
THOM: All the rich could die and Jan'd never shed a tear.
AND: Of course; if all the city died, you'd then be heir—
    Since your father loved you so he made you a city's
     ward.   350
THOM: And three to one that Jan was knocked about the head:
    Ah, yes, see how he stands there glumly, quite besotted?
HARM: But see here, Jan Knol, Thomas is a bankrupt:
    'Twould be ill for him, could he not declare each year or
     five.
JAN: He's a very eelskin hawker. Come, my man,
    Weren't you bankrupt last in Westphal?
    I avow that you ran off without paying the good folk there,

And you were forced to leave your land.
It's all true—it's written in the books,
But Charles V has made decrees that touch on such as
    you,*   360
What ought always to be done to such as you.
Those articles are printed in large letters.
Would you like to see them, base cheat? Just walk up New
    Bridge,
And look across to Vollewyk. At the gallows there,*
There hang those articles with all their seals.
THOM: Ha! You've snared yourself! How do you know the way
    so well?
JAN: No, Thomas, I'm no bankrupt. What could you mean?
What's all this to me? Had I but one friend in all the world,
And if he falsely played the bankrupt, I'd hang him if I
    could.
A thousand little thieves are hanged   370
Who steal because they're poor, who've hardly stolen a
    pea.
Now, insolvency can come to man by accidents at sea,
Or by mischance—for these all sorrow—
Or a man who's cheated by's bookkeepers or cashiers—
These deserve our pity.
THOM: That's certain, yes.
AND: Are you mad, Jan Knol? Why're you so angry?
JAN: I say that willful bankrupts should be banned from off the
    streets,
And in their exile, far from their wonted haunts,
The boys should throw dank mud at them—or other
    things.
AND: But Floris, how many dead this week?   380
HARM: About as many as last week, maybe less—
But why ask me? Ask the churchyard gossips:
They stand there the whole afternoon and talk of little
    else.
There stand the busybodies, group by group and flock by
    flock.
Elsie Koockleckers is there; Styn Snoeps has her basket
Full of chestnuts and turnips; they munch and pare.
Yonder on a stoop stands old Liz droning her beads,

Mumbling so quickly that it seems she wants the endverse
    badly,
Her old gums moving fast as a trotter's arsehole.*
Then, she's hardly done with beads when they begin upon
    the dead;   390
They know something ill of everyone.
It's: "He was a womanizer; he a rogue; he a rake —
Tsk, tsk, but think, our Lobbich is the bride
Of Harmen Gladmuyl — and his wife not one month dead!"
"Oh, don't I know! Wasn't Janny Stronx her bridesmaid?"
"Lord," says Nellie, "Klassie Boelen is very worldly
    dressed "
"Oh, immodest! Oh, uncouth! Oh, everything she owns,
    she wears!
A silver keyring, a light blue dress, and what a shawl!"
So says crazy Niesie, foul-faced and full of spite.
You'd piss with laughing if you'd seen her.   400
"Child," she'll say, "she's such a testy one — watch out for
    her:
Such a gossip, such a rumor monger — can't conceal a
    thing."
In that she'd quite resemble Niesie. She tells more than
    she knows.
AND: Floris Harmensz, is all this true?
HARM: Wabbie Klonters* knows it all:
She sits there on a bucket, taking note of all that passes —
'Tis why she speaks so sad and knowingly.
She knows exact how many dead I've carried to a grave,
How many men in weeds of mourning,
How many women too, how many wear black veils,*
How much white bread on rich men's trellises,*   410
And, Andries, so much else that there's no end.
Now I'd do best to quit. I could go on about these loose-
    mouths.
JAN: My friend, you can't quit now —
You must say something of the old men too.
THOM: Yes, forget the bier a moment — what about the men?
You must also tell of them.
HARM: I've much to do. My time is short. No long theme now,
    But under the clock at the New Church, there sits a gaggle

Of old codgers, old jokers, wags, old bachelors,
With hanging heads, hunch-backs, and crooked shoulders;
There sit the drip-noses, eyes arunning.   420
Thirsty Frankie says: "Mieuwes, you're nigh eighty —
I know 'cause you and I, we went to school to Master
            Floris,
Licentiate* of Amersvoort — remember Kackedoris?
The fellow was cracked, though he was sure that he was
            wise.
Remember when he came into van Dieman's garden?
And thought he was in Eden? And when you convinced
            him
You had a rabbit big as an elephant? That it bore calves?
Oh, a thousand things: how you had an eel so long
That when England saw his head, his tail was on our
            beach?"
            How the old crumps titter over any bit of
                                    ribaldry: 430
Whenever there's any in the air, they all come to hear.
Old Jan Selde tells how he was asked to dance
By the oldest harper in Amsterdam — what was his name?
            Jan Vlas?
Or tells how his father, in a rage, shut him up one day.
What'd he do? He climbed out over the fence,
And fetched Frans Wittebrootd and Jan Treck, who were at
            a wedding.
They bought from cesspit tenders there a tub or two of
            shit,
And this they put in sacks and piled it on the stoop —
All that delectable, perfumed ambrosia —
And then the rascals hid, with fingers to their noses.   440
An old uncle soon came feeling through the dark: he
            tripped, he fell,
He screamed, he sneezed, he nearly choked — you'd all
            have crossed
And blessed yourselves to hear how he did curse and they
            did laugh.
"Wait, wait," they said. "We've still a use for this!"
And so they rudely knocked upon the door,
So rudely that the wedding guests all came streaming out,

And fell, baptizing each the other in that mustard.
They floundered in that sugar tart, just like I know not
        how,
And soon the slop was flying by the fistful;
'Twould be the time to find a sheltered corner.   450
Well, those old crook-backs could write books, on and
        on—
Nay, 'tis true—I heard it with these same ears.
Adieu, Jan Knol, Andries, Thomas: I must go:

> [*Exit Jan Knol, Andries, Thomas, Floris Harmensz.*]
> (*Enter the two boys, Joosie and Kontant.*)

JOOS: Marbles! Who wants marbles? Six for a dime!*
KON: We'll shoot for a few, or I'll knock you.
JOOS: 'Tis well enough. Come on. Put your four in.
    Come on, let's have your hat. Oh, yes, I'll take you on.
KON: What'll it be, my friend, even or odd?
JOOS: Even then.

> [*Joosie lobs.*]

KON: One's out, Joosie! See seven are left.
JOOS: Well, come on. It's alright with me—we'll shoot for all
        eight then.   460
    Go ahead and shoot, if you've the strength.

> [*Kontant shoots.*]

    How many out . . . let's see. Now there are four in.
    Ah, dearest knothead—you'd better quit, or I'll win 'em all.
KON: You play dirty—I'll watch your hands!
    Come on, foulert—we'll play for five.
JOOS: Let me go first. Well, all right. I'll give you a shot.
KON: What gibberish. I'll give you a knock!

> [*Kontant shoots.*]

JOOS: Oh, blood—what a shot! The marble had a flat spot too.
KON: Well, my marbles'd mourn if I lost all the time.
JOOS: How many'd you knock out?
KON: One, and all the rest to come.   470

> [*Kontant shoots.*]

There's another out! I'll show you.

JOOS: So you say. 'Tis but a pair. My turn now.

[Joosie shoots.]

KON: Now mine.

[Kontant shoots.]

JOOS: Now to get your big one — then you've lost them all.

[Joosie shoots.]

Got it there!

KON: No you didn't!

JOOS: Now it's mine!

KON: It's not!

Now give me all my marbles back, my friend. Look now —
How'd you like a nice bald fist?

[Kontant hits Joosie.]

JOOS: God's pains — that's foul!

[Enter Floris Harmensz.]

HARM: Come here, you scoundrels — I'll teach you to fight!

[Floris Harmensz catches the boys and beats them.]

You ruffians, take that and that!

KON: Oh, it's murder!

[The boys escape.]

JOOS: Old cripple, puss-nose, halt-leg!

HARM: Catch the do-bads! Catch those boys! Rapscallions! 480

KON: Hey, Joosie, my man, let's go find old ropes
And throw raggedy-arse down upon his cheeks.

HARM: Where are they gone? They were just here —

JOOS: Dear old cripple, do you think we care a pickle's wart for
            you?

HARM: Oh, let me catch you, let me catch you! I'll beat your
            skins!

[All three run out.]

ACT II

(*Jerolimo and Robbeknol*) [*before their house.*]

ROB: I've won no prize here either* — can't keep house,
    Not here where hunger's baked and thirst is brewed.
JER: 'Tis ill indeed — you've not once brushed
    My mantle or my jacket. See, they're quite spotted.
    Come and look, man. You must immediately brush
        me.   490
    And have you no brush?
ROB [*aside*]:   And have you no hog's feathers?
    None in the house.
JER: What's all that you say?
ROB: Oh, nothing at all, my lord.
JER: Straighten my collar then;
    And get my red-plumed bonnet, lad,
    And my sword; go get water, page,
    And a clean washcloth and the gilded ewer.
ROB [*aside*]: How the fellow rails. Well he knows he doesn't
    Even own a broken pot.
JER: Why do you chatter there?
ROB: See, master, here's the cloth and water.
    Anything else, my lord?
JER: It cannot much become me   500
    To answer such a one as you.
    You'll do as I say, obeying my commands.
    Fetch me now my ivory comb. I must see to my hair.
ROB: There's your comb for you. If my eyes see right,
    'Twas once the tail bone of some oily fish.
JER: How very droll. How are my locks now?
ROB: They curl like grapevines; I do not jest.
JER: What think you of my hair? Is't not fair and lovely?
ROB: Oh, quite like an English rabbit, dappled as 'tis with
        gray.
JER: How sits my bonnet? And my elegant feathers?   510
ROB: Master, your cap's astride three large curls —
    It's wondrously affecting.
JER: And how's my ruff?
    Is it right for me?

ROB: What a question, master.
Your apparel suits you so well, in such comely wise,
It seems your mother formed you in the womb to wear
            such clothes.
JER: Ah, Robbeknol, this sword, it is so *excellente* —
It once belonged to the old Wolf* himself.
ROB: I never knew him.
JER: I'd part with it for no sum, however great,
For master Thomas never made a better.
See here how perfectly it pares this bit of fingernail?   520
I'd wager that I could hew a sack of wool in half.
ROB: Not near as well as my teeth could hew rye bread —
Though 'twas a twelve-pound loaf, I'd destroy it.
JER: 'Tis a lovely piece of work — but what? It's through the
            sheath.
ROB: Perfect for a courtier — it well becomes a nobleman.
JER: I'm going out to meet our sexton and pastor.
I forget me — ah, yes! Now where's my wooden rosary?
ROB [aside]: There goes the poor blood proudly out,
A very Genoan, pretty as a bride.
JER: Well, *Robbért*, now make the bed; I'll trust the house
            to you.   530
Haul water, be watchful that nothing might be stolen.
Should you go out, do shut the door and lay the key
There upon the ledge, that I might enter when I come,
And be careful that the rats don't get our stores!

                        [*Exit Jerolimo.*]

ROB: If a mouse should happen in, he'd starve.
How grandly he struts; such elegance.
Wouldn't you think he was his highness' self?
Or at least one of his council? So haughty's his ap-
            pearance.
God, you send the disease, but then you send the cure.
Whoever saw his lordship walking spry and brisk   540
Would never think he'd not a penny in his purse.
He who seems so courteous and cheerful? Who'd ever
            know
That he's eaten neither yesterday nor today —
Excepting a wedge of bread I bore here beneath my
            shirt,

Which served me as my pantry — and that was gray
    with mold.
Oh God, your works are wonderful.
Who'd not be fooled by such a show of weal?
His lordship approaches, discoursing like a prince
Who lacks nothing, as though all's according to's pleas-
    ure;
He's well decked out and not afraid to brag,   550
Quite as though he had a thousand pounds a year to
    spend.
Who'd think between the two his bed and bolster
Aren't worth a dollar? — nay, include all else he owns.
Could any guess that every morning he wipes
And dries his hands and lordly face on any mildewed
    rag?
No one would believe it! But Lord in heaven
Only knows how many such there are in this world
Who'd suffer more for idle honor and display
Than for God's holy laws. These besotted wills,
'Tis such a feeble glory that they seek,   560
But it sometimes bankrupts life and soul.
Well, my thoughts have gone a'wandering again;
For certain I was nigh translated to a higher sphere.
Now I'd best go in and shut the door —
I suppose I've got to do my work.

                        [Exit Robbeknol.]
      (Enter the two strumpets, Tryn Jans and Pale An.)

TRYN: Nay, lordy, those were noble fellows.
How merrily they flipped their flagons out the win-
    dow,*
All the way across the street. The youngest was a stur-
    dy chap —
God's pains, I've finally had my belly full of dancing —
Truly now, by Jesus' sides, he was a jolly one.   570
God's wounds, I hate these sipping drinkers, these stin-
    gy dogs.
Now, I prize a rich and cultured lover,
But still I say, the servant's better for the tart.
But Annie, tell me, what news?

AN: A pretty Spanish silver piece. I'll buy some lovely
    thing,
  Before it slips through my fingers. That's fine, eh Tryn
    Jans?
  I've such a longing for French slippers.
  I'm driven half mad whenever I hear their clicking
    heels,
  I'll tell you that. I'm frantic for them.
  What did you get, Tryn?
TRYN: A half pistole.*   580
  I lately pawned some things of mine, some baubles—
  There's my pawn slip: read for me how much it comes
    to.
AN: What letters are these? The Devil read it.
  Here an "X," there a curl, a line, *par dieu*.
  This is Satan's script; old Nick himself must have writ
    it.
TRYN: Well, it's my hat for all of that, once I can get it back.
  They write that way so none can copy tickets.
  Say, lovey, come with me to the dye-works,
  To Pockmark Nell* — it's nearby here.
  What's all your shuffling? 'Tis no sin—   590
  The little wife will quickly fetch
  My bodice hooks, my skirt, and hood.
  Just see what tattered rags must hide my belly now:
  I spit when I look at 'em, full of holes and patches.
  And in the mean time, I'll order up a pint or two—
  But why can't you stand still? What excitement's this?
AN: 'Tis on account of a fellow who wouldn't pay before his
    fun.
  He promised me a jacket, two dresses, and a cloak.
  "*Specy in manum*," said I. "God is no deceiver. . . ."*
  "I'll give it to you," said he, "as true as I here stand. 600
  He who gives money in advance," said he, "takes love
    on faith."
  Then says I, "To promise much, lover,
  And give so little is granting joy to fools.*
  That's nothing for my plate," says I. "So, my fine young
    man,

When I see one, I know a knave, as well as he knows
    me."*
And so he paid. I can't tell
If he or I first threw the blanket down,
But well I do know that when I saw him there so
    pretty,

(Enter Jerolimo.)

I thought there'd come an angel to my bed.
Hello, here comes what seems a man of means.   610
Hush! Good day, *signeur.* Do you know the time?*
JER: My little heart's balm, 'tis almost ten.
But Jesus, what bliss! Petite, angelic one,
My golden idol, in loving salutation,
And by your gracious leave, I kiss your slender hand.
Whither wend you, my heart, without a *serviteur!*
TRYN: We stroll, for our pleasure, by the riverside, *monseur.*
JER: Triumphant maids, in virtue and in honor garbed—
Whose eyes alone would quite compel the greatest of
    the world—
The least of all your earthly slaves,   620
Who wishes you all the fullness of your heart's desire,
Does bid your majesties so low to stoop as to allow me
For the slightest moment to share your promenade.
AN: We not only grant your sweet petition,
But we hold ourselves greatly honored,
As well by your person as by your polite address.
JER: Goddesses, you surpass in beauty and in knowledge
Wise Pallas, chaste Diane,
Pale Venus, and the daughter of the swan,
The Spartan queen, who brought as well the noble
    Trojans   630
To fire and blood, as to death she brought the Greeks.*
Oh, queenly lady! Should Phoebus see you,
Heaven's great light would sure be dimmed—
He'd let his swift chariot and horses rest,
To sate and satisfy his *grandioso* desire for you!
TRYN: By your leave, my lord, I can't conceive you.
Is't Portuguese or Italian that you speak?

Your poetizing's much too high for us.

JER: Provincial maid,* how *glorieux* your discourse!
Like waters purling from Parnassus fount,   640
Your lovely words come flowing from your tongue.
For sure you have been suckled by the muses
At the fount of Hippocrene,* and not at mortal's
        breast.
Drudge that I am, how can I conceive of all the gods
Who have their habitation in your mind:
They sing their music in your rhetoric.
Oh, you high Batavian* priestesses of Mercury!
Truly, my lovelies, I had imagined that
My discourse here was not with mortals, but with
        nymphs,
Nymphs who bathe in the Amstel's silver flood,*   650
Nymphs whose sojourn's but infrequent here on land.
But since I've seen you, you little souls of Helicon,*
I'm half convinced you're sisters of Jupiter!
Oh, daughters of divinity, mine own heart's blisses,
        can you
Object to lofty admiration? Oh, beauties, surely not!
Do reply, my princesses; do sing for me.

AN: My lord, have you some new ditty for us to sing?

TRYN: I'll honor you with something sweet when the time is
        right.

JER: I'd like some pretty miss for bedfellow.

AN: That you could have [*aside*] and a fist in your eye.   660

JER: Well, I have a new song, but the key's too high for me.

AN: Well, lovey, let's see if we can sing the piece.

JER: Don't tear it, for 'twas sent me by the Duke* himself.
Were't not a rare piece, he'd not have sent it me.

TRYN: Such high associations—
My lord, sit down and we'll peruse it.

        (*They sing "Betty goes to Mary Mount."*)*
        [*Enter Robbeknol behind.*]

ROB: Well, I've made the bed, and now it's to
The well at Raempoort* to get clear water
In my pot—how now? Can this be?
Well, I'm mad. My master with a brace of trollops?   670

Ah, my good and worthy lord, do you desire to cater-
    waul?
I look myself blind. But good, the man's no fool:
How much wider's the choice with two instead of one.
JER: Well, my dears, is't not a lovely air? His highness'*
    courtiers
Are all quite mad to sing the song.
The Infanta* sings it herself; her maids of honor
Sing it at the court, and cry it in the street.
AN: Is't so, my lord?
JER: Why, little girls of three
Warble it every one.
TRYN: Such wonders that you tell.
JER: Oh, the scamps and rogues, they learn it earlier yet,   680
Earlier than their paternoster, as though 'twere God's
    own gift.
ROB [aside]: What madness.
AN: Shall we arise, my lord?
JER: Oh, damsel, will you grant me one small courtesy?
Allow your humblest slave a little kiss?
TRYN: Don't be naughty now, my lord. Aye, love, be calm.
ROB [aside]: I could laugh me off my feet. How now, shabby
    master?
He follows her like men might follow their holiday
    humors.
JER: I pray you, allow me, if possible, allow me—
AN: Come, my lord, let's to the tavern,
Here on Kloveniers—'tis where all the noble fellows
    go.   690
JER: Alas, I've not the time; I must soon away.
It's nigh twelve, and I must hasten to the exchange.
I've large interests there attending.
TRYN: Well then, my lord, do you but slip us half a piece of
    eight,*
And we'll wait where ever you should choose.
JER: My soul, I know not what to do—if only money
Could be changed for time, and then there's something
    else:
The king himself has written me graciously,
Granting me the office of "King's Coachman,"

A magnificent charge, at once genteel and grand.   700
And so I must regard these taverns too vulgar low
For persons of stature, like myself—surely the *glorieux*
Should not mingle with pimpled faces and low
          wenches,
Gross creatures that they are. A man of high authority
Must only fraternize with those of equal quality;
Thus madam, I must excuse myself.
Considering my estate, 'twould not be honorable.
Those of us concerned to maintain a reputation
Must not approach low folk or wine—
Unless it be to toast a friend's good health.   710
Drink's as great a blow to probity as are loose women.
Gracious *mesdames*, my time is fled;
Je vo bassa la man, de vostre signory. *
ROB [*aside*]: By St. Luke, he's got all the tricks!
The whores curtsy—you'll foul your blouses, with
          bowing so low.
And see how he slings his cap about.
JER: I kiss the flea, madam, which sat upon your hand. *
                                        [*Exit Jerolimo.*]

TRYN: Off with you, you fop.
AN: Go, you balding nit.
Could you follow him?
TRYN: But half.
AN: I, not at all.
I thought at first that God had sent a gentleman.   720
ROB [*aside*]: There goes my master—he wasn't what they
          thought:
That bird's but skin and bone. Tsk, tsk, no sooner had
The strumpets met a likely one than quick they're cast
          a'down.
Now I must go home and clean the place,
But holla—I've not drawn my water yet!
                                        [*Exit Robbeknol.*]

AN: My God, Tryn, it seemed you two would make a happy
          pair.
TRYN: That dog's arse? What? I'll not say the end I'd wish for
          him.
What would the bunghole do? He's naught but talk.

Now my last night's fellow was of another sort.
But Pale An, how long have you been a member of our
     great guild?   730
AN: I've run wild since my fourteenth year:
    I lived away from home, and where I came to live,
    I romped with servants and the master's sons—
    You well know what happens, what comes of wild
        times and folly:
    Light girls are quickly on their backs.
    But hear, I'll tell you how it went, in short:
    My master's oldest son was always pawing at my
        breasts.
    I wasn't angry. I let him do it.
    You see, he loved me, and I too was green—
    Oh, I'd grab him if he missed me.   740
    It happened once that while I made his bed,
    He caught me in his arms and threw me on the sheets!
    I can't begin to tell what fun the fellow had
    Before he had his will. Oh my, such pretty speeches.
TRYN: Did you cry out?
AN: Cry out? What? I nearly burst with laughing.
    'Twasn't bad at all—oh, 'twas sweet.
    He bought me every little thing: a silver thimble,
    Keyring, a purse, a pair of English knives,
    New cloaks, and all of it first class.
    I strutted like a coach horse, proud of my fine trap-
        pings.   750
    I seemed on Sundays more the house's daughter than
        its maid.
    But, alas, it seems no amount of luck can long endure,
    For soon a babbling bunch of jealous neighbors
    Sought out my mistress, who was a simpleton.
    "Watch out," they said. "The cart's not straight upon
        the way.*
    Your maid is spoilt—she has more than's fitting for
        her.
    Your husband gives her all these wares, or else she's
        stolen them;
    Watch your money and your drawers." My mistress
        then accused me
    Of fornication with her wedded mate.

I swore 'twasn't true by my soul, by all the saints,   760
By life itself, so long that she began to doubt,
But nevertheless, their poison still was lodged in her;
For once your heart's afire with jealousy,
You'll not be rid of it through all eternity,
And it's worse with women than with men.
My mistress followed me about the house, and even in
      the street.
Now here's what she did: she conceived a plan
To catch the mouse outside his hole.
She posted one of her nieces to watch my door.
When 'twas night, as was my custom, I arose   770
And went peacefully to my dear to bed me.
The niece came out of hiding, lit a candle,
And followed me there, step for step,
And when she came upstairs, she found the loving
      couple
In all friendliness in bed together.
The mother sacked me, and I had to take my little all
And leave the house; him she sent to Bremen.
'Twas thus I joined our guild. What more can I say?
But how came you to't?
TRYN: I'll tell you; listen.
For five years I served in a house in Nes,   780
And saved my money, and all very carefully.
I earned high wages, and I got gifts
By little usuries more than one would think.
I scraped so much together — for see, I was no spend-
      thrift —
That I could buy whatever I pleased.
So, soon thereafter, I thought to rent a room
And do washing and cleaning in the neighborhood.
So I thought, and so I did — but 'twas heavy work.
I then decided to leave my mistress. She was surprised.
She asked me what was wrong; was it higher wages
      that I wanted?   790
Was I to work for another? What was I about to do?
At last she found that I wanted to live on my own.
Well, finally, there was an end to that.

I went then with my gossip to stay at the Kathuyser's
        inn,
But soon there came a fellow, a young merrymaker,
A son of Zeedike—old Dirik was his father's name.
He talked to me so prettily—we had a glorious time.
We left for Haarlem, where we lodged together
At a splendid inn that served the quality.
As I lay asleep that night, he stole all my money,   800
My silver, and my purse, which was so nicely packed,
And crept silently away, never waking me.
Away upon the wind he was, over the fields and pas-
        tures.
In the morning, Annie, as I fell from out my dream,
I felt for my love, but I found him not.
I called him by his name, and then I sought my purse:
I fainted when I realized he'd run away with it.
The scene I caused can hardly be described;
I had to leave my cloak to pay the bill.
Bewailing my fortune, I went away disconsolate,   810
Down Zylstreet, to Overveen* and out upon the
        downs,
'Twas there a townsman, who had come to hunt, found
        me.
I told him all that had occurred,
And he sympathized with me. I thought him very nice,
And he gave me a French gold crown.
AN: He gave it you for nothing?
TRYN: You can't suppose a Haarlemer
Would give a stranger coins for nothing.
Since then I've bounced from bed to bed—not just any
        bed:
I much prefer your grand *seigneur* to greasy boors.
AN: And you've never heard tidings of the rogue?   820
TRYN: I've heard he's left the Baltic to come home—
Oh, I've served process on him; the bailiff'll catch him
        soon.
It'll cost him his head, were his neck of gold.
AN: How'd he look?
TRYN: Very well, though he was cross-eyed.

Well, goodbye. Hey, there, where are you Nelly?

[*Exit both, Tryn into a house.*] (*Enter Robbeknol.*)

ROB: There's no furniture — it's dirty, desolate —
No broom nor goosewing* to sweep the house.
Oh, it's foul. Look up. Look down:
Everywhere it's full of clods and scabs, spider webs and
      dust.
I wonder that a nobleman   830
Can be content with such a miserable kennel.
Well, what now? Sally forth and hunt some bread?
If I wait much longer, I'll die starvation's death.
It seems my master's quite forgotten me.
And if he never returns, should I then never eat?
No, that's not just — no, 'tis best that I go visit
The great houses. There's naught to gain from such as
      these.
But holla! I have to leave the key,
So when my master comes, he'll not complain.

(*Exit Robbeknol.*) [*Enter Jerolimo.*]

JER: Certes, the common people here are coarse and
      ordinair;   840
They cannot make distinction between an elevated
      soul
And the grossest churl, who's simple, just a fool.
It grieves me that these people are so lacking in the
      graces.
If a prince or duke should come to see this land,
He'd neither get respect nor reverence.
These fools would stand with covered heads and spec-
      ulate,
Allowing royalty to pass unhonored and unnoticed.*
Us Brabanters are an outstanding folk.
We're point polite, superior in understanding,
Eloquent of speech, gracious in honoring the
      worthy,   850
We're all taught manners, quite like the children of a
      lord.
Our least citizen's so friendly and polite,

That he'd not speak rudely to a foreigner;
He might say, "What ya' lookin' for? what ya' want?
Who ya' askin' for? for Peter the learned?
Oh, Lord! He's my chum—here Gilles or Peryn,
Bring this stranger to Uncle Peer's cousin,
There next the Blue Bread Inn, near Hanssen's son's
    grandmother,
There near the beer wharves—" Such noodles, these
    Hollanders.*
And then they're lacking generosity, however rich they
    be.   860
In Antwerp there are none so poor but that at Friday's
    market,
As palms are slapping palms,* their wives don't buy a
    bodice,
Trimmed with thread of gold and buttons too,
And satin dresses, skirts of velvet—
Everyone dresses so, even whores in their bordellos.
A *courageux* people. But here's the key;
My boy is out. I'll unlock the door.
And fold my cloak and lay it in the press,*
And then I'll stroll about the inner garden.
                  [*Exit Jerolimo into their house.*]
            (Enter Robbeknol, eating.)

ROB: Oh, it has its wonted taste. To work, you slender
    cheeks!   870
Now once again you'll show your art and cunning.
There's bacon here to last 'til spring—
Fresh liver, ox snout, good bread, and sheep tripe,
A sausage, a cow's hoof—here's much to guzzle.
I have much to thank good people for.
God's blood, how can I eat it all? My belly's stiff.
I've stuffed in already near twelve pounds of bread,
With an excellent pot of grits.
I'm quite concerned how I might best enjoy the rest.
Forward! As says the wench who would begin again.   880
By all God's elements, what's this? My bakery is weary.*
God's pains, it's late. What shall I do?
It's well past five. Oh, how my lord'll scold.

I'm in for it — oh, my!

[*Enter Jerolimo.*]

JER: Where had you to go?
   Where have you been?
ROB: Don't hit me master —
   I waited longer than two hours here for you.
   I could at last no longer endure my hunger:
   My hollow belly cried that it had lost its skill.
   Thus I threw myself upon the mercy of God, and cer-
          tain people.
   See, they granted me these morsels.   890
   [*aside*] Yes, his face is softened now, not near so harsh
JER: Well, I waited dinner for you,
   But since you didn't come, I supped without you.
   But you've done well, thus to seek your bread,
   For 'tis more blessèd to beg than to steal.
   'Fore God, *Robbért*, I am not angered.
   One thing, I pray you though: do be sure that no one
          knows
   You live with me; for I assure you,
   'Twould greatly lessen the world's esteem for me,
   As I hope to avoid all slightest taint of scandal.   900
   I'm not quite *firmé* established here, you see —
   Ah, had God but willed that I had stayed at home.
ROB: My lord, I needn't blab all this.
   You needn't worry.
JER: Well, eat then, poor fellow.
   Perhaps the Lord will sweeten our poverty.
   Robbért, my lad, ever since I came to this house
   I've had hard times; my life's been harsh.
   This house, it seems to me, was built on evil ground.
   Certes, there are unlucky houses,
   Houses which allow their occupants no whit good for-
          tune,   910
   But rather woe, as this house does to me.
   Therefore I promise you, as soon as this month's past,
   I'll change both this house and my fortune too.
ROB (*aside*): How narrowly he regards my tripe; he's gazing
          at my bread.
   Aye, see, he can't take his eyes off my lap,

Since it's now my table. See how his face entreats me?
I must pity the poor fellow:
I've suffered often in quite the same way.
Indeed, I suffer daily from that which troubles him.
What must I do? Let him eat? I'd be overwhelmed with
        thanks: 920
He says he's eaten, and yet I'm sure
He hasn't had a nibble all the day.
I could wish his pain were eased a bit,
As 'twas yesterday when those crumbs I had,
They served us both a supper.
JER: In truth, dear Robbeknol, you do amaze me.
    You've a marvellous constitution;
    You eat with such tremendous grindings of the jaws
    That you can reawaken appetite even in me.
ROB [aside]: Oh, that's beside the mark—'tis your hollow
        belly   930
And your crying bowels that make you eager.
I know how 'tis: he'd be a glutton if he could.
Well, no hurry, good fellow, I'll show you how.
My lord, if you've a will, set to. This bread is very good,
As is this cow's hoof, and the tripe is, oh, so sweet.
A man could be flat full and still desire these dainties.
If you please, eat up. Holla! Careful there!
JER: Is this the cow's hoof?
ROB: Yes, my lord. Try it.
JER: Such dainties I'd prefer to any turkey hen.

       (He sits and eats with Robbeknol.)

ROB [aside]: Well, what think you? Had he eaten?   940
    He gnaws that bone closer than would a dog.
JER: Oh, this is tasty too.
ROB: The sauce you brought with you—
    'Tis the world's most tantalizing.*
JER: By God, this tastes so good to me,
    It seems I haven't eaten for two whole days.
ROB: Oh, you hit it on the head—as though 'twas true.
    It seems you do good justice to the food.
JER: Now fetch the water home—but watch that you don't
        spill.

ROB: The pot's brim full—none's been taken out.
JER: Go to my chamber then, and take the cover off the
        bed,   950
  And fold my napkin and the table cloth,
  and lay them in the pantry.
ROB: I'll do it well, my lord.
  [aside] Now his pride is up again.
  High words maintain his gravity—
  He who hasn't yet a musselshell to scrape his arse.*

ACT III, SCENE I

[In Jerolimo's house.]

ROB: 'Tis said that he who drinks well, sleeps well, and who
        well sleeps, sins not;
  And he who does no sin will certainly be blessed.*
  Now, I have slept well, and, for once, I've eaten well,
  But I've seen but little bliss.
  My, my, what men on this old earth don't undergo.   960
  Why must mankind endure such misery?
  Does anyone know? Everyone asks, "Why?"
  But all we know is what we all endure.
  What calamities I've suffered,
  Of thirst, of hunger, of what miseries more,
  Floating to and fro from friend to foe—
  And what odd ones that I've served!
  Whatever master I got was miserly and spare;
  The one was always more niggardly than the last,
  And now I've one who gives me neither food nor
        bread—   970
  A master I myself must feed!
  Yet, I like him, for look, 'tis written
  That he who nothing has can nothing give.*

And if I've suffered greatly,
Then all the more should I show sympathy.
      He's walking in his shirt to take his ease,
There behind the house. Now I can search his cloak.
I'll sniff through it once to quell uncertainty.
Holla! I'll look through his breeches quickly;
Now his jacket; now his sleeves —   980
God's death! I've found his purse; it's got a thousand
      folds.
Nothing here, no, no, no, no, no, no — many nothings.
It appears there's been no money here for many a day.
Oh, this one's a needy devil. Well, he's truly,
For his poverty, deserving of my pity.
But I'll hate with right that blind and grasping master
And that unlucky, skinflint priest.
The first, he got his living begging, with me to catch
      his coins;
My Latin earned the other's keep,
And for my service both would let me starve.   990
God knows, I'll never see a young courtier out wandering,
But that I'll wonder, as we pass each other by,
If he's as far from rich as my poor master is.
Well, as I say, he's a better master,
Even in his poverty, than were the others.
But I do wish that he'd admit his state,
That he'd not strut as proudly as he does.
It appears one law is strict obeyed
By Brabanters, by men as well as women:
Anyone with pleats and ruffles is a great lord,   1000
Though, like me, he have no penny in his purse.
Well, may God amend before we're brought to ruin.
But, I fear me, all such'll perish in their sins.
Now, before my master comes, I must go in
And fold his purse back into its thousand folds.

ACT III, SCENE II

(Jan, Andries, Harmen) *[on a street.]*

JAN: *Bon'sjours*, what news? What say you, Andries? Harmen?
AND: Time passes, but not as it ought. The land is full of
    alarums:
  One would have us here, the other wants us there. Bad
    work, bad work.
  And then there's civil strife, divisions in the church—
  If the frog and the mouse stand bickering thus,   1010
  The fox may well surprise them.*
HAR: The world runs in fickle fashion.
JAN: How'd you know, Harmen? What change of fortune
    might you know?
  You came from Twent and Drente, riding on a whisp of
    straw.*
HAR: That's nothing. I'm quite as good as five of the likes of
    you.
  I came to Amsterdam with more than you, do you follow,
    Jan?
  You came bare-arsed; I was clothed at least.*
AND: True, true. Well paid. If you will make sport of for-
    eigners,
  Then I and others too will quickly answer back.
  Oh, dear Jan, if Harmen, I, and others had not done the
    work,   1020
  Then all would not have gone on here near so well.
JAN: Not so bad—say rather that with all our foreign trade,
  We've received many thorough-going rascals.
  Whatever's freighted or transported in
  Is worth far less, God help us, than its cost.
  The old simplicity whereof we often speak
  Has nearly all been throtled by this new deceit.
  Where is faith fled? Holland's trustworthiness?
  'Tis sure 'tis fled so far that your kind'll never seek it out.
  Used to be, one's word was pledge. Now one must write
    with cunning   1030
  To be safe in dealings with these sly rogues.
AND: Who brings more trade and merchandise than us?

JAN: Who bring more lies and rascality than your lot?
HAR: Who brought subtlety to your impoverished wit?
JAN: Who brought the evil to overcome our virtue?
　　Whenever I think on this, I'm sure
　　That we've been slighted in the bargain:
　　Whatever trade we have with foreigners —
　　They'll see to cheat us in the end.
HAR: That's just to say, 'tis best in business to have sharp
　　　　　　eyes — 1040
　　But come, Hollanders are not earth's finest folk.
AND: Yes, it must be very dark indeed before a Hollander
　　Would lose a winding path; I could tell some tales had I a
　　　　mind.
JAN: Yes, Andries loves to tell the worst of folk.
AND: Well, you know your way about a lie quite well enough.
HAR: It seems to me our discourse here
　　Is nothing less than honorable —
　　If I've said aught that might offend, none should take it
　　　　　　personally:
　　Just laugh; assume that I referred to someone else.
JAN: Well, if ill we're going to speak of everyone, 1050
　　We'd best begin here with ourselves.
HAR: That's true; that's just. But Jan, 'tis already known
　　That you're a glutton and a drunkard.
JAN: That may be true, Harmen, but I don't beat women;
　　'Tis well known what kind of house you superintend.
　　And if there's any coupling to be done in town,
　　'Tis sure that Andries here has had his pander's fee.
　　And bankruptcy? Harmen can juggle things to make it
　　　　　　right.
　　You're a very advocate for dishonest causes.
AND: Well, then, let's go round — we've each a turn; 1060
　　Was it long ago you had the pox?
　　Doesn't matter — you still walk that lurching pace.*
HAR: Oh, you've touched him there. We're so concerned
　　　　　　about our friends —
　　Where is that child born to your sister, the nun,
　　She who lept so lightly to the pastor every night?
JAN: And perhaps, Harmen, you'll tell us all
　　Why you were driven out of Ditmaars?*

Was that for your virtue?
HAR: Now stop there, Jan. You go too far.
    You'd surely not, by God, impute dishonesty to me!
    Don't talk so, God's blood! I'm numbered 'mongst the
              pious.   1070
AND: The pious? You resemble more the turd from whence
              you sprang.
    Oh yes, we know you and your family fairly well—
    Who was it that you claim as yours?
HAR: Yes, claim or not, that's no real concern.
    If I could give a tub of gold as dowry with each child,
    I'd wager that 'ere long I'd be sitting on the cushion,*
    That the highest in the land would beg me for my
              daughters.
    Men are these days so scrupulous:
    If there's money enough they'd marry any lazy idiot,
    And even if there'd be no eager Amsterdammer,   1080
    There'd be a Zeelander,* or one from Den Haag—
    However little that they like most Amsterdammers—
    Who'd wed most lovingly an easeful wife,
    Were there but coin enough thereby. Such times are these,
    Were I a Turk or a Jew, I'd be well satisfied.
JAN: 'Tis truth you say—'tis difficult to see aright:
    For there are some so crafty foul,
    That 'tis shameful, no, sinful. Myself, I've seen
    Such things as for my life I'd not thought possible.
    Suffer and avoid,* be silent: 'tis thus that one must
              live.   1090
HAR: Tell us, Andries, what news this morning?
    What's happened yesterday or last night?
    Has anyone been arrested? Raped?
    Anyone disturbed the peace? Any vandalism? Smashed
              glass?
    You're the one who always tries to hear things first.
    You were this morning on the bridge before the sun,
    And there you take the news out of its nest before it flies.
AND: Ah, Jan, just this day I heard
    That excellent, good English beer has come,
    And last evening late, a young maid   1100
    Was ravished by some German on the Haarlemmer dike—

JAN: A German? From Westphalia, I heard it said.
AND: By the blood, he'll be sorry when the sheriff gets him.
HAR: Should the sheriff catch him, he'll buy the sheriff off.
JAN: Yes, the Provincial court won't get much of that.
AND: Rapist? Bah! I've never heard the like.
    The beast. What a villain's that, to rape a maid.
HAR: Oh, dear Andries, uncle, it happens now so often.
JAN: A lord of necks, a hangman there in Haarlem did it once:
    He lost an eye, and they whipped him on the wheel.   1110
AND: He deserved the gallows, according to his lusts.
    Well, foul-mouth Melis had his cheek cut yesterday,
    And our Jan was beat about his arse,
    And Dirk said to Elsie such ugly things
    That no dog would eat them—
    And then she'd throw them back at him, just as she'd
        caught 'em.
    That woman's got the devil or his cousin in her tongue.
    Joost Dirksz left today to sail for Flanders,
    And left his brother Klaas to protect his wife.
    He shuts up the house just as he pleases,   1120
    So that no stranger will enter in by night.
    Oh, Joost's a far-sighted man, he'd have you know:
    He'd have none but Klaas gain entry to the portal.
    Oh, prudence is a virtue.
    Such wisdom Joost had in early youth—
    And Truefool has lost his case in court.
    And the great merchant is saddled now with care,
    And Hillebrant Droochnap has kissed away
    Her silver plate to Elsgen and Prussian Al.
    Thirsty Dirky, he'd never waste his money—   1130
    But now some sharpie's bilked him of it all.
    That little man who goes to all the sheriff's sales,
    To bid the prizes up at all the auctions there?
    Last night they left him hanging with last bid on a man-
        sion.
    And the night watch finally laid their hands on Jan the
        Brawler;
    And madman Harmen has escaped the hospital;
    And our own Hans Jong is about to wed,
    And Brother Karnelis has wed a little thing from Zeeland,

But she hates him now she's heard he's laid some eggs
    away from home.
JAN: Andries, you know everything — where do you find it
    all?   1140
I must believe you hunt above and far beneath the earth.
HAR: What's this I hear? What will this be?
AND: It's the bell at City Hall — some proclamation's to be read.

(Enter Robbeknol with a crowd of people.)

ROB: They're hurrying to the Dam.* What will this mean?
'Tis an execution, sure, for the City Bell is ringing.
I must go too — perhaps a flogging;
If someone's whipped, he'll soon repent him —
But no, the cushions* are laid out. There's the sheriff
With the secretary — see that you hold your tongue.

[The proclamation is read by an official.]

My honorable lords of the courts of Amsterdam: considering the great deceits and concourses of healthy men
who are idle; considering the vagabonds, the useless beggars, the numbers of foreign poor who are in our midst;
considering all these get their keep as highwaymen, as
thieves, by treacherous attacks, by robbery and plunder-
ing; considering their godless gambling, dicing, and the
brawling, drunk-drinking, and whoring; and considering as
well our slender supplies of grain and the slight hope we
have of other grains to come, and the expense* which shall
consequently fall as a heavy burden upon our city, all to
the detriment of our own deserving poor, a statute is here
ordained by my honorable and aforementioned lords ex-
pressly to this effect: that from this day forth no beggars,
vagabonds, idlers, pickpockets, be they old or young,
blind, crippled, lame, or leprous, or what else, shall be
allowed to roam or gather alms in market places, on
bridges, before the churches, at the gates, or on the corners
of our streets. All such vagrants must immediately leave
our fair city, on pain of public pillorying and whipping. My
honorable lords do also decree that no one presume to
molest, hinder, or do violence to whatever sergeants, pro-
vosts, and deputies, as shall be designated to fulfill these

behests, in the execution of their rightful duties or in the
apprehension of willful, idle villains and vagrants, all on
the pains above listed; further, that all the deserving poor
shall be obligated to give their name, condition, and place
of residence to the worthies above named, that those worthies might ascertain the true condition of the poor and see
to their rightful needs. All this is done by the Council of
this city, enacted March 18, in the presence of my Lord the
Sheriff and all the magistrates.*

Brederood.*

[Exit Robbeknol, the crowd, etc.]

AND: What think you, Jan? Is that not well considered?   1150
JAN: There hasn't been a better work in many a day.
HAR: But however good it is, someone will reproach it.
AND: Yes, who? A troop of scum, of felons, rogues, and va-
      grants,
  Or other rabbles of shameless villains.
HAR: No, I mean some honorable folk, who'll have pity for the
      poor.
JAN: That would be an aid to those who lead a riotous life:
  If folk will satisfy the dishonest wants of ne'er-do-wells,
  They'll but persist. It is well, it seems to me,
  To ban these troublemakers from our midst.
AND: But if the poor are thus sent out into the world,   1160
  Where will they come to rest?
JAN: That I'll leave to them. But why are you so hot in their de-
      fense?
  Are you afraid that soon you'll have to leave?
  The people here grow weary, giving so much away;
  They're weary of these rurals and these foreign jabberers—
  'Tis they that pinch our deserving paupers,
  Who tearfully must hawk their shame for bits of last
      week's bread.
  Yes, the Almshouse regents would feed them,
  And twenty of our burghers' children would gladly show
      the way.
  But our poor, they're too proud for that,   1170
  While moffs and poops* are eels just bred to beg.
  Just look along the Rietvink and the Ouwe Wal,

Let alone the Haarlemmerdike. Lord's wounds, what
      crowds of them,*
What mobs of thieves and foularts.
There's hardly a day without its blows and brawls.
Every Friday there come in at the gates new droves
Of renegades and foreign hellions.
All the robust women there have shawls, as though they're
      deathly sick—
Whole troops of them, marching to a silent drum,
Along the Newdike, and so through all our streets.   1180
The people here are givers—'tis plain in all their char-
      ities—
But each one throws away his alms. 'Tis sure 'tis foolish
To give alms to those who, come Sunday morning,
Will gamble it away before the gates,
Dicing with cutthroats and snatchpurses,
Playing among themselves at cards and skittles,
Lobbing marbles, flipping coins, guessing heads or tails*—
What good can alms do them? None, though it be a copper.
It's plain such charities only breed bloodlettings and
      murders—
Yes, murders and thievery. And if they're caught   1190
By bailiffs or by city guardsmen,
And if they come to jail, then do the fishwives
Loudly take the cutthroats' part,
If money and deceit don't quickly blindfold justice.
'Tis all a consequence of foolish charities.
Oh, and none may scoff at these abuses
Or scorn the scum who wastes the alms
And leaves his wife and babes to mourn their hardship.
Yes, they guard against real need industriously.
If Overtoom, Kathuysers, or Sloterdike had power of
      speech,*   1200
What tales we'd hear to fright our ears.
AND: The laborers and teamsters—now there's a troop
    That knows the bottom of an ale can. What think you, Jan?
    Aren't they the connoisseurs? Why a single sip
    Of beer and then they'll tell you whence it came—who
      brewed it too.
HAR: They help to circulate our coin.

AND: 'Tis their shame's in constant circulation.
    They abuse their drink—and eggs and cheese as well.
    Them prosper our land? They prosper the devil;
    They prosper the smugglers of foreign beers.   1210
    There's no excise there for our city's brewers.
    And all the farmers, when they join in,
    The one will steal it from the other;
    But these foreign brewers and their tapmen,
    And those who smuggle beer at night, they lose no coin for
        that.
    And then there are the honest-seeming merchants,
    Who rent cellars to fill with smuggled French and Rhenish
        wines,
    Who bring their vats through back doors secretly,
    To steal from magistrates the proper tax.*
    The magistrates must watch more narrowly,   1220
    Or soon the land'll be impoverished.
    Yes, those with wine on tap—
    They draw it night and day.* If there'd been some one
    To keep their hands from off those taps,
    They'd not in such short time build such great houses.
    Honest folk look on, and sorrow at what they see:
    Their own custom's thus the less, as all men know.
    But truth, it's late. I must go home and eat.
HAR: I'm hungry too. I've had no breakfast.

    [Exit Jan, Harmen, and Andries; enter Robbeknol.]

ROB: God's flowing wounds, what hunger's in our house!   1230
    We're both so still, as still as mice.
    We never speak a word, so harshly we're beset.
    No one knows such need until he's suffered it.
    What shall I do? I can't fancy
    How I am to get our little bread.
    But yet, I'm worried not so much about myself,
    As by my master's plight.
    How will the poor man find the means to live?
    No money, nothing left to pawn, and no one's bringing
        gifts.
    But why prate on like this? By God, he still appears   1240
    As though he'd never felt a touch of hunger.

I know not what he eats, nor can I think
Whom he might visit for a supper.
Perhaps he eats the wind for food, as chameleons do.*
But nonetheless, whenever you see him strolling,
He juts his chin and gazes so about,
Just like a watchful greyhound, slim of limb.
Well, *Robbért*, 'tis time for you to think of means:
None better than the trade I learned so long ago.
I'll go get my Bible out of the corner,   1250
And then I'll get my bread most honorably.

                                          [*Exit Robbeknol.*]
(*Enter Tryn Snaps, Els Kals, and Jut Jans, all spinsters.*)

TRYN S. [*as to one off stage*]: It's not your business, hear you
          cork-dry Jan?*
     Your wife may be a whore, as might your daughter—your
          son's wife too!
     Away you whorehound! Go do it with your turnip peddler!
     Good fortune, piss-thief, that I've not ground you to a
          powder.
     I'm an honorable woman, as good as you or any one!
     Why trouble me? If you're rich, it's in the devil's service.
     My husband romp in others' sheets? You'll learn to hold
          your tongue!
     Come out if you've a liver for it! I'll teach you sheet
          romping!
     Just try to talk of romping now—you've clods for
          balls!   1260
     I'll chop you up and drop you in a pickling vat.
     By my rights, I say again, you'll speak no more of romping,
     Or else I'll reshape that shameless face of yours—
     I tell you, you'll have romping out your arse,
     If there's any justice in this town, by God's wounds!
     You hound's pizzle, come out! Come out your kitchen.
     What though my husband in his youth did once some
          thievery?
     That matters not at all—we're friends for all of that.
     What though he's branded as a thief? He earned it.
     What though I did some trullery when I was young?   1270
     I was young, but I'd wit enough not to call for mother.

Though I was fourteen, I'd been enough for any man for
      months.
And if virtue's path was not my own, by Mary's breast, so
      what?
ELS: Now, Trynie, that's enough, you've given him enough.
Whatever he's said, it's to his sorrow. Forgive and forget.
He's best who does best; don't you know that "whore" is
      but a word?
'Tis no more. Don't let it trouble you.
TRYN S.:   My reputation!
My honor! My honor! My honor! My honor! He must
      make amends,
Or I'll take this knife and widen out his arse.
What though they have my ears in Hoorn?*   1280
What though my dad was hanged? Is that so great a thing?
Many's the righteous man who's hanged. 'Tis no shame—
At least, thank God, he was no suicide,
As are some men. What is it to you?
You who've thieves and the devil's own cronies for friends.
JUT: Tut, tut, Trynie, what talk is this? Why so hot?
If he's done ought or said ought, he'll suffer for it in the
      end.
Don't be so wild. Be still, be still, good mother.
TRYN S.: And what the devil's my younger brother to him?
What though he wants to be a hangman? He'd serve his
      God.   1290
Why might he not apply as well as any other?
He's a citizen—but then it seems the office goes
From one foreigner to the next. 'Tis ever so.
If he conducts him well, he'd be a proper deputy.
But first he must do in the present deputy,
Or play informer for a month of five or six.*
One does not achieve high station at a jump—
Unless you've friends in high places.
Say what you will, but it's an honest office:
He'd serve his God and holy justice.
Oh, and it's profitable! A thrifty deputy   1300
Can save, oh, at least a hundred pounds against his leaner
      years.

ELS: Well, surely that's no little matter. If there's so much to
        gain,
    I wonder that men of standing don't apply.
TRYN S.: What are you doing? Spinning? 'Tis good flax.
    The thread's like silk, and you've a fine quick hand.
    Where do you find your wool? On Newdike or Halsteeg?
    None's left at the flea market or on the Burghwal.
    How dear's the wool? Where do you sell? Or do you work
        on order?
    I have some flax to hackle here and clean.*
    I do it very well, as well as ever Hilda could,   1310
    However much it's shouted that she's the Queen of Hack-
        lers.
    No sooner begun than done — that's what they say of me.
    Those Pigmarket hacklers would burst their laces keeping
        up with me!
    I'm faster than the others; I'm as great as Jan Brown's nose.
    Jutie — if I may ask — are you Baptist, Papist, Arminian,*
    Or Calvinist? What a hubbub now about churchly doings.
    If 'twere left to us, we'd get them all together soon
        enough;
    For though it's I who says it, I may speak hastily,
    But then I'm done. Oh, Mother Mary, yes, I know what's
        right.
JUT: Elsie Kals, think you things'll ever be better in our
        time?   1320
    No, no, Trynie: God's books are difficult to read.*
    The task's beyond us. Wool and flax — there's enough for
        us.
    Elsie, have you any tokens from Newchurch or Old-
        church?*
    The almoners, every week they deal them out to the poor
        folk,
    But people now don't give so much to the poor: now 'tis
        dimes,
    Where once 'twas guilders. The paupers had it better then,
    But now the times are dear, they don't get near as much.
    Look, all the costs are high, but Annie Klaas, she does
        much good,

May God reward her, in the Drie Testen, along the wall
    there.
We'll never know how many arches she rents there for the
    poor.*   1330
And every Sunday she sends greens and cabbage, peas, and
    beans,
And stockfish, porridge: you've never seen such kindness
    to the poor.
Why, if she herself was but a bit of barleybread,
She'd give herself away. A woman of such good heart,
No doubt she'd cut her heart out and give it to another,
If he'd need of it. 'Twas but yesterday she sent cloth
    enough
That Lobberich, Dibberich, and Gerberich each made
    dresses.
One day she brought such a weave of linen;
And what'd she do with it? She parsed it out among the
    needy.

ELS: I know one like her. I must tell you of her goodness.   1340
Oh, how often that she's looked into my cupboard
To see if ought was lacking there, to see if I had need.
A little later there'd come a pot of butter and some bread,
A scuttle of peat, some firewood, a basket of kindling,
A vat of herring, a lovely salted eel,
And salted herring, and then she clothed my children too,
And sent them to the city school, where they'd never been
    before.*

                (*Enter Robbeknol, reading.*)

ROB: Well, enough. Good woman, see how far I've read—right
    to that dot.
TRYN S.: Oh, wonderful! Come here. Do read me a chapter.
But look! Jesus Mary! Lord help me! Is that God's
    word?   1350
I'll be better for hearing of it—never heard it yet;
Don't know A from B: my parents never let me learn let-
    ters.
How prettily the fellow reads. How could he learn it?
Stay a bit, good father, yes, read again.

Any evangelist whatever; you know what's best.
I'm Roman Catholic and go to mass,
But what then? I don't break my head about such matters.
If there's a pope who stands and speaks in Latin, 'tis well,
Though he's none the wiser for it, let alone myself.
Good and bad we should be taught in all simplicity.   1360
Can all their disputations help me know if I do right?
ELS: Now my knight, my lover, lively now,
Do read us one about St. George, nicely from the start.*

(Robbeknol reads from Bible.)

JUT: But father, where do you live? You've learned your letters
            well.
My little prince, do come more often.
We've seen but little of you — hardly anything, hear you,
But see, I'll give you this. Now take it freely, that's the fel-
            low.
You're as good as pork, and pork's as good as gold.
When you come to read, our food's as much for you as for
            ourselves.
ROB: I thank you, good woman. The lord provides;   1370
He provided for the multitude with five dry loaves.*
TRYN S.: Speak on, my little angel-treasure. He's so sweet,
      That I'm sure the loving Lord'll take him up to heaven.
      Come often and stay until the candle's burned a'down.
      What think you, Jutie? Isn't he a very prophet?
      Ah, yes. Come in with me and talk. I've such a pretty fire.
ELS: Well, I'll come in.
JUT: Though I was dead, I'd not stay behind.
                  [Exit Tryn Snaps, Els Kals, and Jut Jans.]
                  (Enter Jerolimo.)

JER: How variable and marvelous are fortune's ways.
      Might any of you good people know if Amsterdam's for
            sale?
      You needn't trust my credit for't; I'll pay with silver
            specie.   1380
      Dear merchants, good people, I am the grandest in the
            land.
      And if these States hadn't so much else to trouble them,

I'd beseech them to pump the Haarlem Lake a'dry,
At my expense. Oh, yes, by Jesus and St. John, I'd pay for
    it.
These Dutch bumpkins think Jerolimo's penniless —
Yes, well, but watch and don't be fooled. Had I remained in
    Brussels,
The Count of Egmont'd given me his sister or his niece,
And yet these fools think I've come
From Brabant to Amsterdam for its *beautée* —
For shame, you clods, make thereof *non mention*.   1390
Have you never known reverence or *honeur?*
Ah, be thankful to Jerolimo, who so lowers himself,
As to honor your town with all the grandeur of his pres-
    ence.
You snot-noses, I've no desire to marry here,
Though the princess, daughter of the king himself, were
    offered me.
ROB: You'd be fortunate to get a cesspit cleaner's wife.
    If 'twere true the mad do harm themselves, you'd be one
        vast bandage.
JER: But Rob, see how the Lord surpasses all our hopes?

[Showing him money.]

See how His blessings flow from out His gracious hand?
Go to the market place: buy meat and bread and fruit. 1400
We strike the devil in his eye, and all his wealthy minions
    too.
What's more — and now you must rejoice —
I've hired today another house. 'Tis far from here.
I'll be no longer chained to this accursed nest
After this month — and Saturday's the last day!
May he who first set mortar to these stones,
And he who hewed this wood be cursed,
For this house has been the single source of all my woes.
This house was predestined for misery and woe.
You must know, by God, that from the hour I came
        here,   1410
I've tasted neither wine nor any bite of meat.
Rest has been a stranger too. And then this house was built
    so badly,

So dark and somber, that grown men quail before it.
Run, run, run, *Robbért*, run! No delay.
Like young dukes now, we'll break our fast.

> [*Exit Jerolimo.*]

ROB: Oh, thank the blessed Lord. Oh, 'tis well done —
But how's my master come upon such money?
Have thanks, thousandfold thanks, oh, Lord of Hosts,
Who can turn sorrow to a timely joy.
How can this money best be spent?   1420
But first, how much is there? I've not once counted it.
It's as though he's had a public auction.
There's that cook there on the Damsluys; if he's ought
    made up,
That would be well — but no, the fellow's much too dear.
I'll go buy a pan-eel from Jannie Hoyschuur —
No, they're always stale; been in the sun too long.
I do love the coddled rabbit Pierre le Son fixes,
But though it's tasty, it's always devilish tough.
I'll just go to Paul's and get a nice venison pastry —
But I've not funds enough for that; they are beyond
    me.   1430
Well, is't to be London beer or Dell wine* in my jug?
Perhaps I'd better not — whenever my lord gets drunk,
He breaks the table up and all the glasses too;
He's a very madman in his cups.
Where shall I go to get our bread? On Vogelsteeg or at the
    Sweetbread?*
That woman there's as dirty as I know not what. Best
    think again.
Wherever I go, I'll sure get lots — who knows when I'll
    come again?
So now I do it, I'll do it properly.
Well, hey, here comes a dead one — a funeral for sure.

> (*Enter a body, bearers, priests, a wife, and others.*)

WIFE: My lord, my life, my husband — what a cross is this to
    bear!   1440
Alas, where do they bear you? To the house of misery?
To the dark abode? The house of the forgotten?

That house where neither food nor drink is known?
ROB: Oh, my, what do I hear? Oh, my, oh my! My pulse it
      races!
The heavens and the earth now sink away —
They're bringing that corpse here! I'm frightened half
To apoplexy. Oh, I'll sure succomb.
Oh, woe! Oh, woe. Death! Death! Death! Death! Fire! Fire!
Help me! Woe and fire! The evil's in Holland.
My lord! My lord! Help me! Help me! Help me! Help me!
      Save me!   1450
The door! To the door, the door, now Rob, or you'll be
      sorry.

[Jerolimo comes out.]

JER: Well, lad, well, what's all this about?
What's to fear? Why do you slam the door so *furieux?*
ROB: Oh, master, it's coming here — I can't guard the door
      alone —
They're bringing a body — yes, truly — to our house!
JER: A body? A corpse? How so?
ROB: I met it in the street;
Its wife spoke: "My lord, my love, my husband,
Alas, where do they take you? To the house of misery?
The house where there's neither food nor drink?
That unlucky house? The house that's sad and dark?" 1460
Oh, oh, they're bringing him here. Come help me hold the
      door!
I'll hold my back against the door and push.
JER: I can't speak for laughing so.
Oh, ah, I laugh myself mad. I can't bear it!
ROB: Yes, you go ahead and laugh — I'll go mad for fear.
JER: 'Tis true, although I laugh, *Robbért*,
You had good cause to construe it as you did,
When you heard the widow speak,
As she laid her husband out to rest.
But now that God's provided for us,   1470
Do run off and get our food. No one will harm you.
ROB: Oh, let them first get a bit upon their way, my lord.
JER: Now, Markolfus,* stop this, fool, what have we now?

Open up the door! Away, you owl's chick, run away!
Get our breakfast—hear what I say?
ROB: Now, master, I'll go, though I tarry a bit.
Who can take another's fear away?

ACT IV

[*Enter Beatrice, on a street.*]

BEA: You must do something to earn your keep as long as you
    do live.
    'Tis plain to me that when I've nothing, I get the same in
    trade.
    Now, when I was young and fetching, I had a drove of lov-
    ers;   1480
    Then I never thought of buying pins and cloth.*
    Though my friends would warn me, oh, I had a lovely
    time.
    But that's why I'm now as you see me here:
    What little things I had are broken now, my clothing
    torn—
    Had I not known some ways and means, I'd long ago been
    dead.
    Oh, when I was young, many a man I had—
    Yes, as many as anyone in town.
    If all my men had all joined hands,
    They'd have stretched from here to Haarlem.
    What think you? Hasn't my little space been nicely
    filled?   1490
    And still I'm Tryn's and her mother's bawd.
    What was it Peter de Wassacher said in his younger days?
    "Beatrice, Beatrice, you know every turn of Love's old
    road."
    Oh, I had a deal of pleasure then—but now it's done.

When I was young, I wondered if it all could ever end,
But now I'm old, they think me the sourest gooseberry.
But, no matter: a bankrupt merchant's the best of bro-
           kers;*
An old teamster can still hear cracking whips!
How clearly I remember when I slept with Govert.
Oh, what a sweet one, that — what didn't he give me.   1500
What madness that we did together.
That's gone too, but now that I can't sport as once I did,
I sure can help other lusty little creatures to it:
I do know how a woman feels; yes, that I do.
Why, just yesterday I got a pretty dress and cup
From Jannie — Flip's housemaid, don't you know? —
Because I helped her aboard of Goyer's ship,
And though he had her in the galley on a cot,
She said that still 'twas nicer than at home.
And didn't I get a broach and cloak from Captain Tys,   1510
For bedding him with little Lys in my own house?
Well, 'tis sure her Jan's no good for her: he can't do more
           than push.
And isn't Nellie Klaas besotted for the younger Jan?
She saunters all the day there round about his house:
It seems she'd gladly do him once a friendly turn:
If she didn't love him, she'd not follow him so.
She'd give half she owns if she could buy the fellow.
Oh, this goes on without a stop.
I'm sure my house is full of girls —
I'm a kind of agent for the dears,   1520
And those I don't hire out, I soon enough get men.*
Why should I hinder the sweet young things from wid-
           owers and lovers?
Such folk, such folk. Pleasure, yes. Marriage, no.
And whenever married men spy out a new girl —
They think nothing of giving me a half guilder for each
           turn.
Oh, 'tis fine. They do love fresh, little doves.
I have here now a girl. Lord. She knows her calling very
           well.
Might any of you here desire the little tidbit?

Do come forward — she'll repay your money's worth, a bar-
    gain.
If I have the goods, why shouldn't I make a profit?   1530
Now this sweet thing, she's got to pay her rent —
But if she'd followed my advice,
She'd not have had to pawn what all she had.
Yes, we must sometimes do that which is unpleasant;
Whether man or God beholds, it must be done.
If I would tell you what folks won't do when need puts on
    her screws —
Well, an afternoon'd not suffice.
But now I must redeem a ring 'twas pawned,
And then to another pawnshop with these rags.

[Exit Beatrice; enter Robbeknol.]

ROB: Was I afraid? Yes, well, that's behind me now,   1540
But my face has lost its color for a month at least.
And my master laughed, which seems strange to me:
I thought the air was full of fire and thunder.
But now I'm home from the market place —
I haggled and higgled my way from booth to booth —
And such prices too. Horrible, horrible.
The best I did was with that black wench there.
She's a pithy one, but if she's sometimes rude,
She'll not speak foul to anyone who's pleasant in his turn.
She weighed out sausages and bacon   1550
As'll be enough for us for eight fine days.

[Enter Jerolimo.]

Well, how now? See I aright? My master's at the door.
JER: *Bonsiours*, welcome. *Bien venu monseur, monseur.*
What do you have? By St. James, is this a chicken?
Or is it mutton? Lord, Lord, how sweet it smells.
My dearest butterball, what all is here?
In truth, Robbeknol, 'tis madness *extremé*.
Praised be the Lord who helped us from out our *tribula-
    cion*.
Go get a Franciscan, that he might say a proper prayer for
    us,

[Jerolimo begins to eat.]

A prayer of thanks to the Mother of the Holy Church. 1560

[*Robbeknol begins to eat.*]

Well, how the fool does vex me—will you rudely go to
    work,
You boor? You should read your paternoster first.
ROB: How can I wait? By the time I've prayed, it might be gone.
    A short prayer, my lord, makes a longer meal.
    Ah, see how much he stuffs away while I must pray?
    Well, my lord, you'll see that I'll catch up;
    You'll get no chance to walk on my toes.
    God's body! What a guzzler! He eats as hungrily as all
    The laborers about the weigh house together on a bench.
    Watch out, you beer haulers—this one eats like a dike
      worker.   1570
    Watch out, heavy Harmen, watch out Nobbie—this one
      never quits.
    What a glutton's this? His belly knows no bottom.
    Look at that—there's never a moment when his hand's not
      at his mouth.
    How dry it all goes down! Not once he's dampened down
      the load!
    By God's red blood, you'll burst yourself, my lord—
    Don't forget, the belly patcher's dead.*
    A bit of barley bread on top will ease your bowels.
    What for wine or beer'd you like to drink, my lord?
JER: Blockhead, serve me with your head uncovered.*
ROB: Truly, friend, you've packed a deal away.   1580
JER: Go fetch some Hollander to lick my finger tips.
    But my good *Robbért*, haven't you drunk a bit upon your
      way?
ROB: The privilege is granted me for the heavy work of carrying.
JER: Now serve the wine. You lardball, how slow you are.
ROB: Oh, yes, wine's good—weak beer'll give you belly lice,
    But not wine. Oh, no. Surely, never, truly.
JER: Ah, now the gods can keep their nectar and ambrosia.
    I'd invite the king—no, the emperor with all his court,
    To such a banquet.
ROB: Yes, now you've had your share.
JER: Now, *mooschacie*,* hand me my golden toothbrush. 1590

ROB: Yes, yes, I'll give you one. Holla! Where's my bag?

(*He pulls out a battered scrub brush.*)

Ah, here I have it. I've got it. Here 'tis, my lord.
If it's the least bit worn, I've got a thousand more.
If you'd have something on your brush, why, chew a waffle
then.

JER: Rob, just as at table it is fitting
That one alternate one's food with sips of wine,
So polite discourse is fitting too.
After I've had my fill now of food and drink,
I might mention, then, by way of conversation,
Something of my birth. The region? There near Hobo-
ken,   1600
Where all of Brabant's fans are waved.*
That I was born of noble blood and great lineage,
I feel, *ow fait*, in the surgings of my courage,
And *primé*, in the gravity of my heart's yearnings:
More than any man on earth, I long to be a king.
For though my father was a pastry baker,
My mother was well limbed and courteous:
'Twas she brought tarts and marzipan to the homes of great
signeurs,
And to captains, colonels, mighty paymasters,
And to the standard bearer, he of exalted station.   1610
Robbért those Spaniards — 'tis a nation *magnafique*,*
Not unlike us Brabanters, all in all:
We both speak flawlessly our mother tongue.
Believe me: I came north because of an affair of honor;
I did grave insult in Brabant to a nobleman.
He did not, you see, greet me with a proper reverence,
When he saw my stately visage out upon the way.
He did address me — but he hesitated first.

ROB: Well, seems to me, my lord, by your leave,
Though he might be somewhat tardy, it is his right.   1620
For as you say yourself, he was rich and noble;
'Tis but proper that first you honor him.

JER: By St. John, I'll not be first to offer up civilities.
Why, I might have done him a thousand obeisences,
While that discivil ass did never condescend

To take my hand and greet me.
Must I always be the first to doff my hat?
What can you think? That the affront doesn't rankle in my
    blood?
I'll always stand upon my honor as a nobleman.
He should consider the quality of my person.   1630
ROB: Are you selling fish?
JER: What do you mean?
ROB: By your leave,
I'd not be so proud, if I were you;
I'd consider it a mark of true civility
To defer to others. I'd want to be the first to bow,
'Fore all to one who's richer, mightier, and worthier than
    me.
JER: Ah, you're so young and thoughtless, knowing nothing
Of the world, or of the paths of honor.
Honor's the greatest good, and more than any earthly
    treasure,
Ought men of honor to desire it.
Know that while I'm little more than penniless,   1640
I am so high of heart, that though
It be the prince, His Excellency himself I greet,
If he do not return my courtesy to him,
Why, when we meet again, I'd coolly wait for him to
    speak,
Or, upon seeing him, I'd simply turn away.

[*Exit Jerolimo and Robbeknol; enter Geeraart Pennypinch.*]

GEER: Five or six times I've sent old Geert my bill,
And truly she's chewed my ear each time.
What though she be my wife? The laborer is worthy of his
    hire.*
These days nothing's done for nothing; if she fumes and
    screams,
That's none of my affair. I've earned it, and I'll not back
    off.   1650
What's hers is hers — just yesterday she got three cents
    profit
On that salt fish that I brought home for two;
She sold it to Aal Maurits there next door for five.

"Getting money's well," says she. "Shall we give it all for
     fish?
'Twouldn't be wise at all," says she. "We can miss one fish.
We'll have our meals," says she. "We've bread, and butter
     too."
With that she shoves a pan of turnips in my lap
And a blue rag with two stale crusts into my fist,
While she tucks a bib up nicely between her breasts—
Oh, she's cleanly: neat and tidy as I know not.   1660
She's got that naturally from her sainted father:
He always claimed the privilege of gathering up the mussel
     shells.
And then of an evening or a morn, he'd scrape his arse with
     them.*
Slovenliness is no blessing, as says slutty Lysie,
And she's a filthy one. She fouls her pants, she does,
And if her nose drips, and if she spews a bit in babbling,
That's not the worst she does: she throws away her snot
     balls.
I wish that I could have them—I keep all my snotballs in a
     pan,*
For who can know? Perhaps they'll turn to silver at the
     last,
If I can play the alchemist with a philosopher's
     stone—   1670
Quicksilver's the very least I'll get, I'm sure.
If my hair gets cut, I gather up the clippings quick,
'Cause Mopsis the ballmaker gives a shilling a pound for
     hair.
The lousy barbers, they sweep it up and save it for them-
     selves.
But what do I do? Collect it from the garbage piles here
     'round.
And should I find a bit of Spanish leather, greased or dry,
I sell it to the shoemakers for as much as I can get.
Oh, I never see a heap that I don't probe.
And should I find old rags, however putrid, foul or bloody,*
I wash and bleach them in the Singel Canal,   1680
And then I sell them to paper makers for paper coarse or
     fine.

Just wait for me: I know I'll earn my bread.
When I was just this high, I gathered candle butts and cher-
    ry stones.
True, that took some searching — didn't matter.
I didn't let it sour me: I'd sell 'em to a druggist, penny for a
    lot.
Two littles make a big;* how well I know it.
Now here I have a sack wherein I keep old bits of iron,
Whatever it is, I'll save it, if it's any good at all.
Soon I'll have my lot of ground piled high with garbage.
Just yesterday I brought Geert three baskets full of oyster-
    shells,   1690
And she's picked up whole quantities of cinders — each bit
    helps.
Now butchers and oil pressers throw out their offal every
    night,
So, 'fore dawn each day I'm there with my old bucket in
    my hand.
Folk don't understand: they think us mad,
Because I give cowshit to my land, henshit to my trees,
Castaway mash and manshit to my swine,
And if I do this to my profit, why let them gossip then.
And now I've heard that tanners buy old piss,
I don't just let my water run whenever I get the whim.
'Tis neatly stored up in my house — a small vat full I've
    got.   1700
And if it smells a bit, so what? I smell it not.*
Money — 'tis the best thing to collect. Whenever we two do
    eat,
We measure out the draughts and count the bites,
And if perchance I eat some bites too many,
She scratches on a score stick so she'll not forget.
Sunday next I'll miss those bites. They're saved for later in
    the week.
Temperance is a virtue. And if we've never had a child,
We've never spoilt a child with squandering,
Nor spent our means for pride.*
I care for my family, and she for her posterity.
What though I've got three tubs of gold from rents?   1710
I'd rather suffer hunger thus than be a poor man when I die.

Oh, you don't know what praise the world gives
A man who dies and leaves something to his family. *
Although I've got a hundred houses in the city
And many acres out among the farms — still I might die
          poor;
During the war my houses long stood empty.
I think I'll walk along the walls and so to Dolhuis street.
People don't care a twig if their rent's past due.

[*Enter Beatrice.*]

Well, who have we here? How're you, old friend? Good
          day, Beatrice.
BEA: Well, old Geeraart, I wish you pleasant day, and good year
          too.   1720
Where've you been hiding? Tell me, old gaffer.
Truly, I'd near forgot your face.
How's your hearing?
GEER: Fair, fair.
BEA: And your digestion?
GEER: Could be worse, not bad, no.
BEA: How's your sight?
GEER: Passable.
BEA: How do you feel?
GEER: My body's full of gout,
Like most old bodies.
BEA: And how's Jan Hagel?
GEER: Jan's like me: he's dry, as dry as sawdust.
Beatrice, he was such a wild one when he was young,
But now he's old and deaf. What a strife the poor man had
With Lysbet Lammerts, his brother's wife — and that Jacob
          Prol,   1730
His sister's husband. You'd not know him, so much he's
          changed.
BEA: Surely he's not thin? He was ungodly fat when he was
          young.
GEER: No doubt — but with such a heartache, a man must lose
          some flesh.
Now, though he lives in Naarden, still he has no peace. *
'Tis no faked relationship: Lysbet's his sister, true enough.

And Prol's his brother in the flesh — no lies can alter that. *
Do you know, little mother, they made the whole thing
      up.
And so they've lost their father's wealth, every cent.
But this they should have known before they tried;
For it is said: what's dishonest won will never make you
      rich.   1740
No, their father's wealth will never see his grandchildren.
How could he hoodwink so many merchants and barmen?
Why, he'd reckon up two cans of beer whenever he'd play
      cards,
And a pint of wine. Madnooo. The cards'll never repay the
      loss.
When they ate breakfast, six guilders soon enough was
      gobbled up.
He's been known to spend a crown on mulled wine.
Now, 'tis no affair of mine, but his maids were pretty,
And why should that have been? A bit of friendly tussling
Could not cost less than eight guilders a throw,
And then some ruffled sleeves, a jacket, kerchiefs on the
      side —   1750
Beatrice, had I done so, I'd not be what I am today.

BEA: 'Tis truth old man: you say it very well.
No, you don't like squandering; you like to lay it by.
How long I've known you — where's your old crony,
Beningie Naninx's sister's grandson? lived at the Spotted
      Lute? *
How he loved to pass the time in taverns, playing cards.
He was what he was, and that alone — a quick-hand cheat,
      'tis sure:
With dice and cards, he did whatever he pleased.
That hellfired rogue did love to see a woman,
And when he spent his money, he thought it but a bub-
      ble,   1760
But what's all this? The fellow spent it freely, that he did —
He never pained a soul; joyful he was.
He made company — everyone'd run to join him.

GEER: Whence come you?

BEA: From the Kitchen at the City Hall, *

Where I had the porter agree that he, on Monday next,
Should bring the tables out for the sale of Monsieur Rokes'
    goods.
For though Egbert thinks that he'll bring action too,
The landlord must have precedence; that's the city's stat-
    ute.
And if Jan Hen wants money too, too bad: his action's late.
I've had the sheriff seize all Rokes' things — I'll get mine by
    law.   1770
His guardians, Janson and Simon Slecht, I'll also not
    forget.
And if Peter Hink wants to sell Rokes' things 'afore the
    Newchurch,
I'll set my lawyer, Bartel, on him with all his laws!
I've got my sheriff's letter and perfect right to all the goods.
Old Bartel's no fool — he'd defend the devil himself,
Though 'tis true 'twas just yesterday he lost that other suit,
But that he did for love of those learned doctors of the
    law —
Why he even slipped them the usual after 'twas decided,
Then mutters that the advocates'll never learn to read,
Nor even spell, let alone learn laws.   1780
He speaks wicked of the Regents better than any rascal
    can,
And how he wrangles in his chambers with his clerks!
Oh, they twit him so that even dunces see it,
And so he'll rage at all his scribblers and penlickers —
To think they stay to copy, penny for a page!
Bartel would be nothing if he lost his mouth.
What a row was that when Master Marten said Bartel was
    mad.
Bartel went and wagered fourteen pints of beer it wasn't so,
But Marten won — proved it quoting Bartel.
Ah, what all I've spent at court pursuing drunk Jan Dier-
    ten;   1790
Yes, he'll be at City Hall as long as I can pay.
'Tis here a consultation, there the lifting of a clause,
Here a certification, and then again a seal,
Here the sheriff's boy, there a deputy, then the sheriff's
    self,

Here the bailiff, then his clerk, so he can do his part;
All in all, money behind, before, and overall.
Oh, I know their ways — my father was a porter at the
    courts.
GEER: 'Tis true, Beatrice, all that you say —
    Just now I'm on my way to see a needy nobleman:
    I rented him a house; he thinks that he'll not pay.   1800
    If my renters don't pay prompt, then I go get them.
    My lease is clear enough that every month I must be paid.
    Now 'tis true Brabanters, they're not quite Italians,
    Still, they're not far behind; they drive me mad:
    Make themselves an early May ' — and pay with bedstraw.
    But I'll see to this one; yes I will, if Geeraart be my name.
BEA: Truly, truly, well, why shouldn't you?
    I myself am here to get some money from a merchant —
    It's not convenient for him to pay as far as he can reach.
    Holla, here's the place, Geeraart.
GEER: Well, Beatrice, me too!   1810
BEA: You knock.
GEER: No, you knock — nice and calmly.

[*She knocks; enter Robbeknol and Jerolimo, Jerolimo behind
    Robbeknol.*]

ROB: Who knocks so rudely? 'Tis living carrion!
BEA: Is my lord not at home, then?
JER: Say, I'm looking to my affairs,
ROB: He's not here.
GEER: Is't possible for me to have a word with him?
ROB: My good man, yes! But 'tis not convenient now.
JER: Say I'm out receiving cargoes of indigo and scarlet.*
GEER: I must speak with him, boy.
ROB: You can come tomorrow, if you will,
    But if you please, don't stand here 'til they come to sweep
        you up.
BEA: Well, that's nicely said, when I've not been paid!
ROB: Not paid, old bawd? Can't your husband pay his
        debt?*   1820
JER: Tell them I'm busy with my cloves and East Indian pep-
    pers.
GEER: Call him lad. Be quick now! You're a babbler.

ROB: You'll not sail before tomorrow, however loud you call,
    old crock.
BEA: You'd speak thus to a man so full of years?
ROB: Witch, beware! I'll whack your body like you've never
    seen before.
GEER: Pickle, open up the door! I can be violent.
BEA: You'd give spiteful words, instead of money as is owed?
ROB: Have I offended? I say but that it's not convenient now;
    He's busy with his brokers, weighing bales at the
        warehouse.
    He jots on each a number and his mark —   1830
    Oh, many's the bluehat and flapcap* that works for him:
    Flemings for packers, lots of others to carry stuff about.
    Like to see him there? Go on — I've got to see a miller now.
BEA: Why, I'm a whore if once we let you go —
    I'll run screaming down the street, 'til all the neighbors
        come to see.
JER: What a beast she plays. Say that they'll have to wait a bit.
GEER: Lad, if you don't call him, there'll be sorrow in the land.
ROB: Well, old gummer, I'm not moved by threats;
    And you, old sell-crack, what have you to say in all this
        braying?
    What's your will, old shit-skirt? You should speak more
        wisely.   1840
    'Tis not well to speak ill of honest folk, old apple hawker.
GEER: Young man, forgive me. If I offended you, it pains me.
ROB: Yes, well, wait a bit, if you please — my lord's not dressed.
    He's washing his hands clean. He loves purity.
    Do stay a bit.
BEA: Well, that's little enough.

[Jerolimo comes forward.]

JER: *Bons jours, Monseur,* and you, my lovely miss, what
    would you?
    In great haste I've come, from my business and affairs.
    Jove, 'twas such a pace, I do positively sweat.
GEER: I think, my lord, you know my errand?
BEA: And you know, *Sinyeur,* why I've come a'visiting?   1850
JER: *Mesyeurs,* you must know my bookkeeping's somewhat
    behindhand.

No wonder then, my credits and debits are somewhat
       askew —
As soon as all my reckoning is done, I'll balance my ac-
       counts,
And when I've ciphered all my gains and losses up,
I'll make all the entries in my current ledgers,
Just as my illustrious colleague, Aert de Cordes* instructs.
GEER: I speak of my money, my lord, not your accounting.
JER: Well, of course, I have no cash — barely enough for my little
      Acts of charity. We merchants handle money but by form.
      Did you think our money could lie fallow? Yes, that would
       be well.   1860
      But look you, what's the matter? Interest every day ac-
       crues,
      On the basis of a ten per cent *per annum* dividend.
BEA: How's it to be? Do I get my money? Or do I take steps?
JER: Ah, little mother, calm now. You'll be paid.
      I'll go to the bourse now and withdraw, let's say, a thou-
       sand pounds;
      Your little sum I'll send to you tomorrow morning early;
      To the half penny, I'll send precisely what I owe,
      Yes, to a half a half penny! Well, is't good?
BEA: How this bald hole does prate on. Come pretty beau,
      when'll it be?
JER: Whom address you thus? Do you know me? What rabble
      are you?   1870
BEA: Who am I? A woman of honor! You're a ruined man!
GEER: Now, quiet, will you? We'll get nowhere thus.
JER: Certes, you're right,
      A rye straw up your arse you'll get — now off, old grinder,
      And you too, gossip, back to hell where you have friends.
      You'll no longer annoy me, that I swear.
                      [Exit Geeraart and Beatrice.]

Robbeknol, I'll grant you now a furlough. I must hence.
Be honest in your dealings; live as behoves a gentleman.
The neighbors'll feed you. If these two dun again,
Tell them I've been called to Kuilenburch and Vianen.*

ACT V, SCENE I

(Enter the spinsters, Els Kals and Tryn Snaps, and Robbeknol)
[on a street.]

ELS: What do you tell me? Has your master gone?   1880
    Without some slight adieu? Well, that's not neighborly.
    I'm sorry about your master, Robbeknol. Yes, I'm sure.
    Would you like a bit to drink? Drink from the wooden
        bucket there —
    I've no silver cup, as have the rich. Now, bravely now, do
        read again.
TRYN: Hungry lovey? Go to the cupboard and slice the bread or
        meat,
    Whatever else you please — it's as much for you as for my-
        self.
    Now St. Antony's Dike is burst near Diemerdam,
    You'd be fixed for life if you could swing a pick or shovel.
    I've pushed many a wheelbarrow in my day.
    I liked the work; indeed, I did it with a will — I'd sing: 1890
    "Oh, the piles are driven in! Oh, the piles are capped with
        tin!
    Still the seagull's shit eats in! Can you push your wagon
        up?"
    Then I'd pull the pin, and there'd be the load;* then shovel
        quick!
ELS: No, if he wants to work, Amsterdam is field enough:
    Go to the City Mason — he'll make you foreman soon
        enough,
    But he's helped so many of these outlanders get work —
    'Twould be better if Hollanders were hired.
TRYN: If you'd friends among the fishers' guild,
    You could ask to get a penny on your chest.* Fish-haul-
        ing's nice,
    Yes, and oh, 'tis so well paid, so well's I know not
        what.   1900

ACT V, SCENE II

(*Enter Geeraart and Beatrice*) [*before Jerolimo's house.*]

GEER: Even when they're rich, I just don't trust these Braban-
        ters —
It's a folk that puts up tremendous front for very little
        rent.
It's a good man who pays well, and a rich man who has
        much —
To trust's to be deceived;* watch your own; faith is small:
The greater the *Monseur*, the greater's our faith in him,
The greater thief he'll be, and the sooner he'll be gone.*
Just last week a bankrupt fled, and folk had sworn he'd
        build a church.
BEA: My good man, people are no longer to be trusted.
Today it's but a race for money; 'tis the world's way.
Can it be a day in Christendom when Drunken Dirkie
Could do such things to Fatty Klaas, to him his daughter'd
        wed?   1910
First the villain whoreson hounds him out the gates,
And then he'll still bedevil his sister's daughter's hus-
        band,*
And oh, much more. I couldn't tell it all if I had hours.
Such deceptions that the coward lecher's done!
Oh, he'll have a heavy reckoning when Jesus comes.
But how are you? Are you weary? Aren't we there yet?
Well, where are my eyes? We're here. Geeraart, neighbor,
        knock.

(*He knocks.*)

Well, Geeraart, perhaps you're used to knock at greater
        houses —
You knock the neighbors wide awake.
GEER: Let's knock again. Are they dead?
BEA: Everyone a mile around'll know that we want in.   1920

[*Enter Els.*]

ELS: What riot's this? You scared me so! I think you're senseless
        mad.

Well, love, what is't? Speak freely now. What do you want?

GEER: I hear you. This house is mine! Be off! Hear that, old beg-
gar-bag?

I want in. Hobgoblin, watch out! Will they never open up?

ELS: Don't rage so. He left today for Vianen.*

See, there's the key. He laid it on the ledge.

And his servant? Him we've sheltered out of charity.

BEA: Where are you laddie? Come see the light of day, come on.

[*Enter Robbeknol.*]

Where's your master gone?

ROB: He's on the Utrecht barge.*

GEER: Where's he going?

ROB: Do I know?

GEER: What more can happen?   1930

You'll tell me, boy, or by the elements, your skin'll get a
thrashing.

ROB: Can I tell what I don't know?

GEER: I'll go get the sheriff —

Watch now Beatrice! Hold this rascal 'til I return.

He'll be finely whipped once we get him to the inner
chambers.

Neighbors help this woman; if he escapes, I'll tell the
sheriff!

I'll teach him, that I promise, and now to

Master Johannes Pillorem, the notary,

So he can draw us up an inventory of the house.

BEA: Aye, come straight back.

GEER: I'll never hesitate a moment.

[*Exit Geeraart.*]

ELS: Ah, good wife, by God's will, let the poor lad go.   1940

Why punish him for what his master's done?

BEA: Let him go? Let him go? I tremble to think on it.

ELS: Now, calmly, little woman. Tush, tush. Come in here 'til
they've gone.

[*Exit Els, Robbeknol, Beatrice; enter notary and clerk.*]

NOT: Have you the book of protocols? Have you misplaced it,
Jan?

CLERK: It's all here under my arm. All's here, go on.
　　Where do we go, master? To the host at the Three Mops?*
NOT: We'll go with the excise officer to count the wines.
　　Now follow me in comely fashion, for it behooves
　　A notary to move gracefully from place to place.

　　　　　[Enter Geeraart, with two witnesses.]

GEER: Ah, that's him now—what luck is mine.　　　　　1950
　　How grand he looks with that big book. He's reading as he
　　　　walks!
　　Ahem! Ssst. Ahem! Fuw! Oh, poop. I call for naught.
　　Again, ahem! It appears that he comes but little to the
　　　　bourse,
　　For if a man just sneezes there, everyone'll look at him.*
　　You there boy, or rather, you young man! Call the notary!
　　Ah, my friend, whistle so long 'til he hears you.
CLERK: Master Jan, there's a man'd speak with you.
NOT: Well, old friend, *bon jours!* What would you?
GEER: A certifyment or attachment attestification—
　　What do you call it? I forget. Let me see, how was it?　1960
NOT: My good man, I must go to write a will; you cannot detain
　　　　me.
　　A man is on his death bed—he waits but for the notary.
GEER: But you must come with me now and do an inventory!

　　　　　[Passes money.]

NOT: Well, I'd sooner go with you than in ought aggrieve you.
　　I'd not have gone with you had it not been of such import.
GEER: Now, where would the sheriff be? With Annie Klaas at
　　　　the Horn?
　　Or with the host at the Munnekedammer?*
　　He's such a loose one, that's his manner.
　　Well, I speak of him and here he comes!

　　　　　[Enter the sheriff, with deputies.]

　　Good day, Lord Sheriff! Since it's your high office　　1970
　　To help each injured party in right and justice,
　　I pray you'll come away with me, so I can open up—
　　With your consent and presence—a house I've rented out.

SHER: Well, why? What's there to do? And where is this house?
GEER: Lordship, some no-good rented it, and now he's gone,
 But 'fore he comes again and gets his things by night,
 I want it taken into proper custody—
 See, here's the witness and notary all present.
SHER: I'm off to apprehend some money-clipping counter-
   feiters—
 They've not only tampered with king's mint; they've de-
   based the coin!   1980
 They'll be boiled in oil when I've caught 'em—beheaded at
   the least,
 Or have their hands chopped off and torn apart: can't be
   less,
 And then we'll nail a coin to the placque there, as is our
   law.
 There's another gang of *Geusen*,* lusty devils,
 Who disturb the common peace with all they perpetrate,
 To the detriment of mother church and her inquisition.
 I must go catch 'em in the furtherance of godlike justice;
 For see, the Spanish Council's declared,
 Judged, and doomed them to the water, fire, and sword.
 They've got to go—I can't delay on this.   1990
 Weeds don't spring up as fast as these godless rascals.
 Just yesterday another *Geus* hymnal* was on the streets—
 Now there's a taunt to all of our divines,
 The Roman pope, and everyone in Amsterdam—
 Nay, to the king himself, a *crimen laesae majestatis.**
 This protestant scum off there in Hoorn and Enkhuis,*
 They're the ones to blame for all of this.
 I've orders now to get those books, and I mean to get them
 Before the bookbinders have sold them off to all the town.
GEER: Noble lordship, come and help me first.   2000
 Johannes Philorem, for God's sake, say a word.

    [*Geeraart gives notary money.*]

NOT: Lord Sheriff, perhaps I can persuade you?

     [*Money passes.*]

 Do it for the poor man. See how he stands perplexed.
SHER: Well, *dominus notarius*, lively now, and follow me.

GEER: If it please the sheriff, he may lead the way.

[*All exit.*] (*Enter Balich, the pewtersmith; Jasper, the
     goldsmith; Joost; Otie Dickmuyl.*)

BAL: Well, Joosie; well, Jasper! Is that you?

JAS: Well, Balich, are you mad? You ask as though you couldn't
    see.
    Don't you believe your eyes? I wonder at you.

BAL: Mad or not, these eyes, they see a great deal
    That's difficult to understand—right Joost!   2010

JOOST: 'Tis true, 'tis true, Balich: father's nose is mother's joy.*
    Well, where are you off to? Out to get a pot of beer?

JAS: It's always drinking time, say Otie, is it true?

OTIE: Well, I'll not say yes or no. I don't know.
    Don't know properly. Oh, I drink a can or two,
    If it's convenient. Yesterday I had some fun with friends.
    I'd have never believed that Floris'd cheat so much at
        cards,
    And he as dull as anything—'tis sure, 'tis hard to credit.

JOOST: Where were you? There by mother Joosten? or with
        mother Huygen?
    Or at Spotty Meyn's? the Mirthful? or the Gilded Ser-
        pent?*   2020

JAS: Seems to me you know all the inns for miles around.

OTIE: Well, Jasper, is that so queer? Wouldn't I know 'em?
    Haven't I seen my life go by in taverns?

BAL: There's true distinction. Yes, you're a great one.
    Otie, if you'd another set of legs, you'd be a beast.

OTIE: How holy now! Shall I tell you something, Balich?
    You're a very priest; surely you're half in heaven already.
    Your religion's beer-sucking, you don't have to tell us.
    True, you go to church—where saints are staves, all bound
        with hoops;
    Where communion wine's a river down your gullet.   2030
    Tell us, Balich, where's the best beer smuggled in the city?
    On St. Nicklas Street or on the Dirk van Hasselsteeg,
    There where you can get a beer a farthing for a pint?
    Oh, you can drink your share, however thin you be—
    'Tis why you go with shearers, wherever the stuff's the
        cheapest.

There on St. Jacob's Street? on the square? am I right?
On the Beerwharf? in the Nieuwe Stadt, on the Waal, and
    everywhere,
Wherever smugglers cheat the excise men.
The foreigners get double wage at honest folks' expense.
I could say more, were I the tattling sort,   2040
But the rascality of some will surely out at last.
Well, Balich, leaving? Where to?
BAL: I've rented a man nearby some pewter plates and cans and
    cups
And one tin tabletop — I'm going to get my money,
And make sure all my wares get back to me.
And where go you?
JAS: Nearby to get my tapestries,
And my gilt leather hangings — and get money from him
To cover their hire, if he doesn't want to keep them.
It's been a month already since I rented them.
OTIE: I go to see a Brabanter, a grand *monsieur.*   2050
I brought him a few pieces, panels, paintings to examine.
They're nicely painted, well grouped and finished:
Some ancient subjects too, both clothed and nude,*
And if they please him as much as they do me,
And if I can make the sale, I'll win a good amount.
You see, I left him quite a lot:
A figure by Lucas van Leyden, one by Albrecht Dürer,
One van Heemskerk, and a Holbein, one Bandinelli,*
Another of the strife between Hercules and Cerberus,
Oh, and many other things as well, antique as well as
    modern.   2060
I'd not have left so much had he not been plainly rich —
Oh, I left enough to stuff a hall
For any prince or wealthy gentleman.
Well, that's where I go. Let me see, what was his name?
Ah, Signeur Jerolimo — these account books are so handy.
JOOST: Well, the man lives not far from here. You'll not go
    wrong:
I've done for him two little pedestals, a chalice,
Silver plates and matching cups,
A dozen spoons, and salt shakers — two or three.
I sent him them in all good faith.   2070

I'll ask him now if he will keep them.
Well, what crowd is this? Why, there's the sheriff.

[*Enter notary, sheriff, witnesses, the clerk, Robbeknol,
Beatrice, Geeraart, the spinsters.*]

SHER: Well, open up the door.
GEER: What's stopping you?
BAL: What is all this?
TRYN: The man's a bankrupt.
JOOST: Bankrupt? Bankrupt? May God preserve me.
JAS: The devil — has he fled?
SHER: Why do you push! Be calm now!
OTIE: My lord, can't I in honor get what's mine?
SHER: Yes, or no, I know not. You might, you might.
JOOST: Well, can't I say with perfect right what's mine?
BAL: I'll get at mine, though I have to fight you all for it!   2080
SHER: My good man, you can't adjudicate these things yourself.
    That's why we have judges, and their verdict is
    That though the goods be yours, the landlord gets first
            paid.
JOOST: Lord Sheriff, please believe me: I but loaned these things
            to him.
    I did it when he came here fresh from Brabant,
    Did it in good faith. I had no slight foreboding —
    If now I've lost my things, 'tis the devil's doing.
OTIE: Lord Sheriff, I did but leave my paintings on approval —
    To see if later he might want to buy them;
    I brought them just for him to see;   2090
    He hasn't bought them, not at all!
    There are paintings here from both my grandmothers.
SHER: Well, never mind if they're entrusted goods;
    You've now no right to them.
GEER: It's all mine! It's on my ground!
BAL: The rope around your neck'll be yours too, old dog.
    You'll give me all my pewter, or you'll regret it,
    I do swear, for all your life!
OTIE: Give me my paintings — hear me, old slave?
GEER: Do I wrong you? We'll see this in the courts!
JAS: You Susanna-jumper,* will you hold my tapestries?   2100
    My gilded leather and the rest? If so, I'll smite you dead!

GEER: I'll remember that! You're my witness, sheriff.
SHER: Stop now, all of you! In all respect, be still.
'Tis all in city's custody. Who'll say no?
I'll warn you once, don't touch the man,
Don't fight, and don't stand disputing each your claim;
'Twould be better if you left it to the judges.
Now open up, and I'll go in—I'll warn you not to wrangle.
GEER: Well, let's go in. Now, notary, write lively now.

(They search the empty house.)

JAS: The devil plays a part in this—the whole house,
     empty!   2110
BAL: By the sacraments! Oh, death! God's flowing wounds, but
     this looks ill.
OTIE: You little rogue—where have you stashed my paintings?
JOOST: Where are my plates and cups? my salt shakers?
     And all the silver things? Urchin, tell me!
ROB: God knows.
JAS: Where are my wares?
ROB: Do I know?
OTIE: I'll be a madman soon—
     The boy makes sport of us and still walks free.
BAL: Where's my pewter?
ROB: For all I'd guess, some pawnshop,
     Or at some thief's fence.
JAS: Now, sheriff,
     If you please, come, you and your deputies,
     To take this knave, for sure he's privy to these doings. 2120
     They took it all away in dark of night.
SHER: Seize him, Meyndert. So, pickthief, come with me,
     For this time you'll be my prisoner.
ROB: Oh, smiling Jesus, oh!
SHER: You'll be in prison soon enough.
ROB: Oh, spare my life! Let me go—I'll tell all I know.
SHER: Speak up and have no fear.
ROB: Good sirs, now listen: the goods are all his own.
     He told me so himself, those were his own words.
     Good sires, my lords, he said he owned it all,
     And a great estate and a house with its own dove-
          cote—   2130

But now it's fallen into disrepair.
GEER: Notary, now write that down. Get it all down neatly.
It can't be too bad—if only he's worth
As much as he owes me.
NOT: And where is this estate?
ROB: As I understood him, 'twas in Brabant.
NOT: Well, that's the end.
SHER: That's a certainty.
GEER: Where's he from?
ROB: Where? Near the village of Hoboken,
Near Antwerp there.
NOT: From whom is he descended?
ROB: I don't know—his father I suppose.
SHER: A lovely answer, yes.
NOT: 'Tis sweet, eh gentlemen?   2140
This account should very near content you,
Though his debts were twice the which they are.
His father! His father! Oh, I'll die laughing!
ELS: My lords, by your leave, the lad is not to blame—
Oh, he's simple, harmless, innocent,
And so we pray you to excuse him in his youth,
And know he'd not even been with the man for long.
He knows no more of these affairs
Than you or I or anyone.
Just today he came to us complaining of his poverty.   2150
JUT: Sometimes he'd get from us a bit of bread,
Or something else to eat, and then he'd go
Back to his master's house to sleep;
The boy knows nothing of all this—ah, dears, let him go.
The lad has done no harm. I'll vouch for that.
SHER: Ah, but gossips, don't you know that there are many
                    rogues about
Whose hearts are not the like their outsides show the
                    world?
This one's a cunning rascal—full of artful deceptions.
TRYN: Lord, sheriff, he's an innocent.
SHER: Well, I'll let him go.
ROB: I thank your lordship mightily!
SHER: Quick! Get out my sight!   2160
                                    [Exit Robbeknol.]

BAL: If I catch the bankrupt, I'll repay him heartily.
JAS: By God's bleeding limbs, if I just could cut his throat.
    'Tis sure I'm ruined, as God in heaven knows.
JOOST: Who's heard such tales in all his life?
    If I had the fellow now, I'd surely slice him through the
        heart.
    I'll send our 'prenticed goldsmith searching round the
        other shops,
    But 'tis doubtful anything'll ever be returned.

                                                   (*Exit Joost.*)

OTIE: Well, may God amend your losses. I too must take my
        leave.
    I'll follow the thief from one place to another,
    Plague him from one city to the next;   2170
    I'll either get what's mine, or he'll be jailed.
BAL: Well, my fury rages, but I'll not shout it—
    'Tis but a mean thing to cheat poor folk like us.
JAS: There's naught to do but pray for Joost:
    The more you mourn another's loss, the less you feel your
        own.

                              (*Exit Otie, Jasper, and Balich.*)

NOT: Who's going to pay me for my inventory?
SHER: Yes, come forth and give me my wage.
    What are you waiting for? Be quick, give me my money.
BEA: I promise, you'll get no cent from me.
NOT: Come, good father; will you pay my fee?   2180
GEER: What for? You've scribbled naught for me.
SHER: Come now. Come on. Pay my coming—don't drag this
        out.
GEER: I don't owe you anything. You've done nothing.
    Now if you'd caught and jailed that pick-thief,
    I'd pay your fee all mildly—with pleasure.
SHER: Now, reach deep into your purse; don't keep me longer.
    For I've left important matters to do your will in this.
NOT: Myself as well—why hesitate?
    Quickly now, give me what you owe; we've moped here
        long enough;
    Don't hold me any longer; come now, make it good.   2190

SHER: Let your money see the light of day, else I'll use the law.
　　You'd summon me and then refuse to pay?
NOT: If you didn't want me, why'd you come to get me?
　　Now pay my clerk, and give me mine.
GEER: We don't owe the slightest mite—
　　Now give us our copy of the warrant.
NOT: It's not yet done.
BEA: 　　　　Ergo, I've no responsibility to pay—
　　How is it? What could you mean, my friend?
　　Think I'll give coins that you've not earned?
　　I'm no such fool.
GEER: 　　　　These are immodest claims.　　　　　　　　2200
SHER: Now pay me. I can no longer dawdle here.
NOT: And I've been absent from my chambers now so long,
　　It's neither right nor reasonable to be so beastly cheap.
　　I came to serve you here and left more profitable matters
　　　　　go.
SHER: How's it to be? Are you fools? I'll make an end to this.
　　Antony, take that bed and bring it to our jail.
BEA: Criminals! What you do is naked theft!
　　Put it down, I say, and leave it down.
SHER: Well, call me 'fore the judges, if you think you've what to
　　　　　say.
BEA: Is this justice? This is violence!　　　　　　　　2210
SHER: Either I take this bed or you must help me to my
　　　　　money—
　　Of course, *madame*, if you'd drop by, you might work off
　　　　　your debt.
BEA: Are you a sheriff? You're a wanton bed-presser!
　　You murderer of chaste souls! Foul bloodsucker!
　　Oh, you ruffian! If I once catch you, by my soul I'll—
　　But that's not to the point. You're a sheriff? You a sheriff?
　　Yet you'd play the wanton? Little boys'll hoot you down
　　　　　the street,
　　If such little uglinesses ever come to light.
　　　　　　　　　　[*Exit sheriff, clerk, notary, deputies.*]

　　Now I'll go home. I've chapped my arse indeed.
　　　　　　　　　　　　　　　[*Exit Beatrice.*]

GEER: Good day Beatrice, now I'll go my way too.   2220
    I'll just think my house has simply stood there vacant for
        the time.
    Goodbye neighbors, farewell! Consider what you've seen:
    The eye can well behold a man and know him not at all.*
                                        [*Exit Geeraart.*]

ELS: How oft we're fooled by fair appearances.
    But it's small matter to old Geeraart, with his tubs of gold.
JUT: But those who hurt the poor with tricks like these,
    These I'd wish a taste of Emperor Charles' ordinance.*
            If there's any here who think that we touch you,
    We'll change it all according to your pleasure —
    If you'll do us one smallest little favor: 2230
    Write down just how it ought to be, from first to last.

            [*They exit; enter Robbeknol.*]

ROB: Gentlefolk, whoever you are, was this play to your liking?
    If you mourn neither time nor money spent,
    Then show us happily — just do as I do:
    If we've pleased you, all together shout, Hurrah!

Completed in April, 1617.   G. A. Bredero
                                       All is changeable.

Notes

The Dedication to Jacob van Dyck

2 Jacob van Dyck (1567–1631) was born in Haarlem, was ambassador to the Netherlands from Sweden, 1612–20, and was founder of the city of Göteborg, Sweden, in 1621. A vivacious man, he is said to have preferred parties to administration. See Helge Almquist, *Goteborgs Historia*, vol. 1 (Götteborg, 1929).

7 This is only traditional, since Gotland had been a Danish possession since 1570. (See Stutterheim's note to this line in his edition of the *Spaanschen Erabander* [Culemborg, 1974]. Hereafter all references to Stutterheim's notes will simply be designated "Stutterheim.")

9 This is in the south of Sweden.

26 That is, hearts like van Dyck's.

31 Daniel Heinsius (1580–1655) was born at Ghent. His family moved north during the time of the Catholic persecution. He became one of the most famous of the Renaissance Dutch scholars. Further, see introduction.

47 Presumably these would have been mainly the strict Calvinists, or Counter-remonstrants.

To My Obliging Readers

19 Proverbial. See Pieter J. Harrebomée, *Spreekwoorden der Nederlandsche Taal* (Utrecht, 1870), 2:87.

55 These censorious ones would have been the strict Calvinists. Their opposition to the "indecencies" in *The Spanish Brabanter* might have been as much inspired by their politics, which Bredero and the Academy opposed, as by their literalist tendency to assume that any play that mentions the indecent is indecent.

85 Proverbial. "Scabby sheep bleet the most." Harrebomée, 2:239.

G. A. Bredero to the Reader

48 Proverbial. "The bee draws honey out of the same flower wherefrom the spider draws his poison." Harrebomée, 1:56.

65 Bredero is playing on the proverb that was a part of the seal of the Netherlands Academy: *Fervet opus, redolentque thymo fragrantia mella (One works here happily, mid the honey smells of thyme and scents of spring.)*

79 "All is changeable" was Bredero's motto, first coined in his second play, *Griane*. See Geoffrey Cotterell, *Amsterdam, the Life of a City* (Boston, 1972), p. 96.

The Argument of the Play

25 Amsterdam's Guardhouse also served as a public house at this time.

44 The seven penitential Psalms (6, 32, 38, 51, 102, 130, 143), the Psalms that were thought to be particularly effective in awakening a sense of sin.

62 See note to line 1764.

64 Proverbial, Harrebomée, 1:27.

Notes to the Play

7 Jerolimo means that the slime is fruitful in the way that the Nile's slime is fruitful. We can assume that he is deaf to the delicious ambiguity.

12 Antwerp was surrounded by defensive canals which derived their waters from the Scheldt. It is in this extravagant sense that the Scheldt reaches the Meyr, a street that begins at the canal on the opposite side of the town from the river. See maps, figures 52 and 53, in Howard Saalman, *Medieval Cities* (New York, 1968).

16 Antwerp's bordello area (Stutterheim).

27 Sleeves were at this time often separate articles which could be worn with any garment.

29 All these Amsterdam creditors come to claim their own in act V.

41 This proverb was inscribed on a scutcheon on the stage (Stutterheim).

46 A "robbeknol" was a fat, foolish lad.

47 See line 170.

66 Proverbial. "He comes from Embden, God help him." See A. A. Verdenius, "De Spaanschen Brabander," *Tijds. v. Ned. Taal en*

Let. 44 (1925):260. Fynes Moryson, *An Itinerary Containing his Ten Yeeres Travell* . . . , 1:87–88, is a chilling contemporary account of this cold, marshy, uncomfortable town.

67 This taunt has not been satisfactorily explained.

71 That is, born in Friesland. Alkmaar is some twenty miles northeast of Amsterdam.

73 That is, she earned her way by walking from farm to farm with a studbull (Stutterheim).

81 Proverbial. "Hold some and give some." Harrebomée, 3:27.

87 The signboard for an inn.

90 The Duc d'Alve, that is, the Duke of Alva (Stutterheim). Alva was one of the most hated Spaniards in the Netherlands.

105 Bits of porkfat would be stuck into the dove to make the bird juicier. A snipe's innards were sometimes taken out, ground fine, and then replaced before roasting. See F. A. Stoett, "Aanteykeningen op den Sp. Brabander," *Tijds. v. Ned. Taal en Let.* 27 (1908):229.

159 The Dutch proverb is, "One mustn't throw the club after the ball." Harrebomée, 1:29.

177 In Bredero's day, the Flemings were considered culturally superior to the Dutch. Even Jerolimo is temperate in comparison with Johannes Becanus, who, in his *Origines Antwerpiane* (Antwerp, 1596), pp. 534–38, proclaimed that Flemish was the language of Eden. See Verdenius, p. 261.

184 This redundancy—"*non paréel*, No comparison"—is typical of Jerolimo's proud attempts at high style. See J. W. Muller, "Nog een en ander over Bredero's Spaanschen Brabander," *Tijds. v. Ned. Taal en Let.* 44 (1925):298.

187 The common European starling mimics other birds, and can even mimic speech.

198 Leyden's university founded in 1575; Louvain's in 1425.

207 For Land Jewels see the introduction. Jerolimo here almost certainly refers to the most famous such competition of them all— that held in Antwerp in 1561.

211–12 Matthys de Kastileyn (fl. early sixteenth century) was a member of the city of Oudenaarde's *Pax Vobis* chamber of rhetoric. Anthonius de Roovere (d. 1482) was called a "Flemish doctor and spiritual poet" by the editor of his *Rhetoricale Wercken* (1562). He was the most famous member of his chamber of rhetoric in Brugge. Cornelis van Gistellen (fl. mid-sixteenth century) was a member of Antwerpen's "Golden Flower" chamber of rhetoric. Klass Kolyn was supposed to have hailed from den Bosch, but he is evidently a fictitious figure, though he would have been real for Bredero. Henryk van Wijn was the first to doubt his existence in his *Historische en Letterkundige Avondstonden* (Amsterdam, 1800), p. 142. Jan Batiste Houwaart (d. 1586) was a famous Brussels poet in his day and something of a mathematician. All of the above is from P. G. W. Gijsbeek, *Biographisch, Anthologisch en Critisch Woordenboek der Nederlandsche Dichters*, 6 vols. (Amsterdam, 1823).

215 That is, a refrain poem, a poem consisting of a number of strophes, all of the same (fairly large) number of lines, all with the same rhyme scheme, all with the same end line (Stutterheim).

217 The rondel was a verse form that originated in France, containing usually fourteen lines and two rhymes. Rhyme scheme was typically a-b-b-a-a-b-a-b-a-b-b-a-a-b. A two-line refrain must also be repeated three times. The ballade originated in Provencal literature. It required three stanzas, an envoy, and a refrain appearing in the last line of every stanza.

218 That is, peasants who write poems—or poets who write about peasants. Bredero, author of the *Book of Peasant Songs*, was himself one of the latter.

220 These are either the names of poems, authors unknown, or simply the kind of expressions that were common in the poetry of the southern rhetoricians.

239 Probably the "captain" was Columbus.

240 See note, line 281.

246 St. Galpert's Eve would be on July 11, three days before St. Bonaventure's day. The latter was a lucky day because Bonaventure's name was etymologically associated with good fortune (Stutterheim).

253 Dantzig, Poland; Rostock, in northern Germany.

269 Impolite terms for Germans.

280 Proverbial. Harrebomée, 1:102.

281 "The Brothers of the Blessed Virgin . . . formed a guild that had an altar in the Old Church. . . . In line 243, however, Jerolimo claims that he'll hear mass in the cloister with the nuns whose cloisters were situated on the Kloveniersburgwal and in the Doelenstraat. He will thus in one morning hear masses in two widely separated chapels. In 1617, neither these cloisters nor the Brothers of the Blessed Virgin existed. Bredero evidently wanted to achieve an easy impression of a Catholic Brabanter in old [Catholic] Amsterdam" (F. A. Stoett and B. C. Damsteegt's edition of the *Spaanschen Brabander* [Zutphen, 1967], p. 29).

287 J. W. P. Drost, *Het Nederlandsch Kinderspel voor de Zeventiende Eeuw* (The Hague, 1914), p. 93, distinguishes between several kinds of marbles which were in use in Renaissance Amsterdam: those which were made of stone; those less evenly round, made of clay; and those even less round, made of the heel bones of pigs or cows. It is the latter, *kooten*, that the boys throw at Floris. As they throw them they are pretending to play a game with him, probably the game wherein the object is to guess whether the uneven *kooten* will land face up or down (Drost, p. 104). They pretend that Floris has guessed wrong—he's thus "lost his bones." Their dialect, however, allows them a nice pun at Floris' expense. For them *kooten* are *klaauwen,* which can also mean "claws," so poor old Floris has also lost his claws; that is, he cannot hurt them.

Since Floris is church beadle, his concern is understandable. There were many statutes which forbade children playing marbles in the church yard (Drost, p. 102), largely because of the danger to the windows of over-enthusiastic play.

295 That is, he will whip them with a whip made out of a stretched and dried bull's penis, a weapon frequently resorted to on such penal occasions.

307 Evidently known for drinking many pints of beer.

315 That is, the plague.

319 Proverbial. "Whoever's name is on the roll, it'll cost him his head." Harrebomée, 1:74.

320 Proverbial. "There's no [curing] herb grown for death." Harrebomée, 1:146.

322 Texel is an island off the northern coast from which so many ships sailed that fugitives were virtually safe from the law (Muller, p. 301).

324–25 Proverbial. Harrebomée, 2:248.

360 Such a decree against willful bankruptcy was issued on October 7, 1531 (Stoett and Damsteegt, p. 57), with death by hanging being the penalty. See lines 2226–27.

364 The gallows stood across the Ij (an arm of the Zuider Zee) from Amsterdam, on a spit of land visible from the city. The gallows can be seen on the lower margin of the beautiful sixteenth-century map reproduced in Georg Braun and Franz Hogenberg, *Old European Cities* (from the *Civitates Orbis Terrarum*), ed. Arthur Hibbert and Rithardt Oehme (London, 1956), p. 50.

389 Proverbial. "His mouth goes like a trotter's arse." See Carolus Tuinman, *De Oorsprong en Uitlegging van . . . Nederduitsche Spreekwoorden* (Middleburg, 1726), 1:197. This is another compendium of Dutch proverbs.

404 Her last name would mean "dirty tricks" (Stutterheim).

408 Though I preserve Stutterheim's line numbers, I take two lines here to translate one of Bredero's.

410 The windows of the rich had been supplied with iron trellises since the middle ages, when they served as protection. By the seventeenth century they were objects of beauty and display. The rich would often sit at their open windows and pass alms to the poor through these trellises. See J. E. ter Gouw, "Taal en Zeden onzer Vaderen . . . ," *Noord en Zuid* 26 (1903):145. There was also the custom of setting out bread for the poor when there was a death in the family. See Stoett and Damsteegt, p. 60.

423 A licentiate was one who had received a license from a university or college, in this case, to teach.

454-74 There is some question as to how these lines ought to be apportioned between the two boys. I have chosen to follow the edition of Stoett and Damsteegt here rather than Stutterheim. P. Leendertz, *"Spaanschen Brabander, vs. 455,"* *Tijds. v. Ned. Taal en Let.* 38 (1919):313-15 provides a nice explanation of this confusing passage. According to Leendertz, once Kontant has bullied Joosie into playing with him, they decide how many marbles to play for—four apiece. Then Kontant's hat is placed on the ground (sometimes a hole was dug for the purpose), and Joosie chooses even and Kontant odd. Joosie then lobs all eight marbles at once toward the hat, the winner being decided by whether there is an even or an odd number inside the hat after his toss. Since "one's out," there are seven in, an odd number, so Kontant wins all eight.

Then Joosie manfully challenges Kontant for all eight, and so Kontant must now lob sixteen marbles (his own eight and Joosie's eight) at once—a lot of marbles for a small hand ("Go ahead and shoot, if you've the strength"). Not surprisingly, not many of the marbles make it into the hat, so Joosie, who started to count those outside the hat ("How many out . . ."), decides instead to count those inside the hat ("Now there are four in"). Since the number is even, Joosie wins all sixteen.

I think a second game begins at line 465. My guess is that this second game is some variation on shooting marbles out of a circle drawn on the ground. Certainly such games were played in seventeenth-century Amsterdam, for which see Drost, p. 98.

517 This whole business of the history of the sword would have been recognized as a part of the romance tradition (Stutterheim). The reference to the old Wolf is obscure, and probably this is the point, since Jerolimo is so haughtily certain of the old Wolf's fame.

567 A manly drinker would hold the tankard with his teeth alone, arching his neck more and more as he drained his drink. When the tankard was empty he would throw it over his head with a snap of his neck (Stoett and Damsteegt, p. 70).

580 A small Spanish gold coin.

589 Pockmark Nell was an *inbrengster*, one who procured such small loan business for Amsterdam's Lending Bank (Stutterheim).

599 *"Specy in manum,"* money in hand; that is, pay in advance. An assumes Tryn's familiarity with the second half of the proverb, "God is no deceiver, but men are" (Stoett and Damsteegt, p. 72).

603 Proverbial. Harrebomée, 1:215.

605 Proverbial. "One knave recognizes another." Harrebomée, 1:65.

611 If the Renaissance traveller, William Brereton, is to be believed, Tryn and Pale An are no more forward than their sisters under Venus: in a "fair street" in Amsterdam there "swarmed the most

impudent whores I have ⸱   eard of, who would, if they saw a
stranger, come into the midc   . the street unto him, pull him by the
coat, and invite him unto the   .ouse." See *Travels in Holland and the
United Provinces, England,*   *;otland, and Ireland* (London, 1844),
p. 55.

631 That is, Helen. Bredero is, of course, parodying conventional
love dialogues.

639 I think that the most reasonable explanation for this expression is one made by Frank Sellin in a personal communication:
"Jerolimo here addresses a street walker as if she were the allegorical
Maiden of the Province of Holland—an allegorical representation
typical of policital paintings depicting Amsterdam and even the
United Provinces as a nude virgin. . . . Jerolimo is used to have fun
with the tradition." But see Stutterheim for an alternate interpreta-
tion.

643 Hippocrene was the fountain of the poets at the foot of Parnassus.

647 Batavia was the Roman name for what is now the Netherlands.

650 Jerolimo's fantastic imaginings are hard at work here, for by
the time the Amstel reached the banks upon which these three
walked, it was little more than an open sewer. See *The Travels of
Peter Mundy in Europe and Asia, 1608–1667*, ed. R. C. Temple (London, 1925), 4:74, for a typical traveller's response to the considerable
stench.

652 Helicon was the habitat of the muses.

663 The reference is probably to the hated Duke of Alva (Stutterheim).

666 Though the tune has come down to us, the text has been lost.
See A. E. H. Swaen, "Betteken voer naer Mariemont," *Tijds. v. Ned.
Taal en Let.* 60 (1941):306–307.

668 Located between the present day Rusland and the Kloveniersburgwal (Stutterheim).

674 Presumably Philip II (Stutterheim).

676 The Spanish princess (Stutterheim).

694 That is, a coin worth four, rather than eight, Spanish reals.

713 This is Jerolimo at his garbled best. He is trying to say
something like, "I kiss the hand of you ladies." His version mixes
French, Spanish, and maybe a bit of Italian.

717 Bredero thus associates Jerolimo with a long line of lovers
who either envied a flea's death at the hand of their beloved, or envied
the liberty the flea enjoyed about the person of their beloved. See
H. David Brumble III, "John Donne's 'The Flea': Some Implications of
the Encyclopedic and Poetic Flea Traditions," *Critical Quarterly* 15
(1973):147–54. Bredero also allows a pun, since Jerolimo's dialect has
him say *hont* for hand, perilously close to the Dutch for dog, *hond,*

since the *d* and *t* sounds are the same in the final position. Stutterheim suggests that there would also have been a pun on *kont*, which is close enough to the English cognate to obviate explanation.

755 Proverbial. Harrebomée, 3:356.

811 Zylstraat, in Haarlem. Overveen is a village to the west of Haarlem.

827 A goosewing would have been used as a duster.

847 Amsterdammers were famous for just such democratic tendencies as Jerolimo deplores. See, for example, Fynes Moryson's account: "And as they love equality in all things, so they naturally kick against great eminency among them . . ." and "no people of Europe . . . useth lesse Ceremoneyes and Pompous Shewes. . . ." See the edition by Charles Hughes, *Shakespeare's Europe . . . Fynes Moryson's Itinerary* (New York, 1967), pp. 369, 379.

859 It would seem that the Dutch were as willing—and able—to speak with foreigners in the seventeenth century as they are today. See Lodovico Guicchardini's account: "An infinite number of those that never were out of the countrye, besides their owne language, speake French, and many Allemaine, Italian, English, Spanish," *The Description of the Low Countries. . .* (London, 1593), p. 14.

862 When a deal was made on the market place, those involved in the transaction would slap each other's palm.

868 That is, a press designed to keep pleats straight.

881 That is, his mouth is tired.

943 That is, hunger is the best sauce.

955 The poor, in fact, did use fragments of mussel shells as we use toilet paper (Stoett and Damsteegt, p. 92). See lines 1662–63.

956-57 The original is a bit of mock logic from Hendrick Spiegel: "Whosoever drinks well, sleeps well; whosoever sleeps well, is no sinner; whosoever does no sin will achieve salvation. Therefore whosoever drinks well will achieve salvation" (Stutterheim).

973 Proverbial. Harrebomée, 3:26.

1011 This is a reference to a Middle Dutch version of an Aesop fable (Stutterheim).

1014 That is, he came in an impoverished condition.

1017 That is, because Jan was born in Amsterdam.

1062 One of the symptoms of syphilis.

1067 An area in the west of the Ducy of Holstein.

1076 The cushion was the symbol of office of the city's Regents.

1081 That is, one from the province of Zeeland.

1090 Proverbial. Harrebomée, 3:45, but the proverb has a particularly rich history. See the first chapter of G. R. Crampton, *The Condition of Creatures* (New Haven, 1974).

1144 Amsterdam's great central square.

1148 See note for line 1076.

The Proclamation

10 Amsterdam was a warehouse city, and one of its most important commodities was grain. The Amsterdam merchants stored immense quantities of grain, which they liked to hold until times of shortage, whereupon they sold with large profit.

32 There was just such a proclamation made on December 16, 1595. It set forth that beggars could beg in certain places only, and then only with written permission from the city. See W. F. H. Oldwelt, "Het Aantal Bedelaars, Vondelingen en Gevangenen te Amsterdam . . . ," *Genootschap Amstelodamum Jaarboek* 39 (1942): 22. There were other similar proclamations in 1596, 1597, and 1613, but there were also facilities set up to meet the needs of the poor. See J. J. 'I'. Poederbach, "Het Armenhuis der Stad Amsterdam," *Genootschap Amstelodamum Jaarboek* 18 (1920):70–142. Altogether, Amsterdam's policies and facilities for the poor, as well as the city's freedom from beggars, were sources of wonder to visitors. The response of James Howell (1619) was typical: "It is a rare thing to meet with a beggar here . . . and this is held to be one of their best pieces of government; for besides the strictness of their laws against mendicants, they have hospitals of all sorts for the young and old . . ." (*Epistolae Ho-Eliane* [Boston, 1908], pp. 20–21).

33 The reference must be to Count Hendrick van Brederode, who did in fact issue a proclamation in Amsterdam in 1567. This proclamation had to do with the watches kept in the city, and with the proper conduct at the city's gates, all in response to the numbers of foreigners who were coming to the city, especially from Brabant and Artois. There was no reference to beggars and such in this proclamation, however (Stutterheim). The Count van Brederode had been one of Bredero's father's heroes. In fact, when the family moved to the house on the Oudezijds Voorburgwal, the "father had the portrait of Brederode hung up as a house sign; and this was the origin of Gerbrand's name" (Cotterell, *Amsterdam*, p. 94).

1171 That is, Germans.

1173 The reputation of the Haarlemmerdike had not improved by 1635, when a special sheriff was appointed to rid the area of "thieves, whores, and other rogues." See C. J. Gimpel, "Onze Oude Dichters en de Amsterdamsche Topographie," *Genootschap Amstelodamum Jaarboek* 12 (1915):98–99.

1187 All of these games would have involved wagers.

1200 Overtoom lay just outside the city. Overtoom, Kathuysers, and Sloterdike were neighborhoods with many inns (Stutterheim) — areas, then, which would have had a large number of foreigners.

1219 These taxes were considerable. See Moryson: "they give tribute of halfe in halfe for foods and most necessary things, commonly paying as much for tribute as the price of the thing sold. . . men pay as much for the impost as for the wine" (4:464).

1223 That is, without the tax being paid.

1244 Because they were observed to spend so much time with their mouths open, it was thought that chameleons derived their sustenance from the wind (Stutterheim).

1252 See note for line 1912.

1280 That is, her ears were cut off as a punishment, presumably for lewd conduct. Hoorn is a town north of Amsterdam, on what was then the Zuider Zee.

1296 I take two lines here to translate one of Bredero's, though I preserve Stutterheim's line numbers.

1309 The hackle was a kind of wire brush which split, straightened, and combed flax fibers in preparation for spinning.

1315 That is, Remonstrant, for which see the Introduction.

1321 Proverbial. Harrebomée, 1:66.

1323 A stamped token given out by the almoners, wherewith food, clothing, or fuel could be obtained (Stoett and Damsteegt, p. 114).

1330 Behind Amsterdam's city walls was a walkway which was supported by arches. Since these arches were large enough to be habitable, the city allowed the needy to use them as dwellings. The rich could also rent them to give to the poor, as does this Annie Klass (ter Gouw, p. 20).

1347 According to Guicchardini, the Amsterdammers "all have some smakering of their grammer and everyone, yea every husbandman can write and read" (p. 14). Of course, he exaggerates, but his amazement at the degree of literacy in Amsterdam is not unusual in travellers' accounts.

1363 Bredero is poking fun at the Catholics as being illiterate and so backward as to confuse the Bible with the books of Saints' lives.

1371 John 6:9.

1431 Perhaps a German wine (Stutterheim).

1435 That is, at a bakery with a sweetbread depicted on its sign (Stutterheim).

1473 Markolfus was an ugly rustic with a quick tongue who appeared in the early sixteenth-century *Dialogue or Disputation between Solomon and Markolfus*, for an edition of which see *Nederlandse Volksboeken*, vol. 7 (Leiden, 1941).

1481 That is, she gave no thought to supporting herself, for example, by working as a seamstress.

1497 Proverbial. Tuinman, 2:115.

1521 She is a *besteedster*, a woman who helps girls find places as domestic servants. Like many of her professional peers, Beatrice also functions as bawd.

1576 Proverbial. "The belly patcher's dead" (i.e., don't eat so much that you burst your belly, because . . .). Tuinman, 1:350.

1579 See lines 950–54. It would seem that it takes no more than a meal to puff up Jerolimo.

1590 From Spanish *muchacho*, "boy" or "servant."

1601 Hoboken is near Antwerp. At the beginning of the seventeenth century, processions were made wherein the pilgrims carried staffs with paper fans attached to them (Stoett and Damsteegt, p. 129).

1611 Brabant was under the control of the Spaniards.

1648 Evidently Geeraart hopes to be repaid for his sexual labors in his wife's behalf. Bredero is punning here on I Cor. 7:3–5. See line 1820.

1663 See note, line 955.

1668 There is a related proverb: "He is so generous that he allows the poor to scrabble for his snot balls." Tuinman, 1:168.

1679 The bloody rags would have been those used to staunch the menstrual flow.

1686 Proverbial. Harrebomée, 1:262.

1701 While the collecting of snot balls and urine might have been a bit extreme, most of the rest of Geeraart's collecting was common enough even as late as the nineteenth century. See Henry Mayhew's chapter on "Street Finders" in *London Labour and the London Poor*, vol. 2 (London, 1967). But to recognize that such collecting was common is, of course, not to deny that Bredero is using the pursuit of trash as a way of talking about avarice — much as Dickens was to do in *Our Mutual Friend*.

1708 I take two lines here to Bredero's one, though I preserve Stutterheim's line numbers.

1713 Except, as he himself has just said, he has no children — he is as barren physically as he is spiritually. He evinces the same confusion in line 1709.

1734 Naarden was a heavily fortified city.

1736 It is unclear exactly what has befallen Jan Hagel (see note, line 1912), but it does seem that his sister Lysbet and his brother Jacob are somehow involved in an incestuous relationship, and that somehow all three have lost their inheritance.

1755 An inn.

1764 The City Kitchen was the quarters for the Warden of City Hall, where in the sixteenth and seventeenth centuries the meals for the members of the city government were prepared. Legally seized goods were taken to the City Kitchen to be sold in order to provide money for these meals (Stutterheim).

1805 May was the month when the leases expired.

1816 That is, expensive dyes.

1820 See note, line 1648.

1831 These would be carriers belonging to two different carriers' guilds.

1856 Aaert de Cordes Jansz (b. 1527) was an Amsterdam schoolmaster who taught bookkeeping—as well as French, German, Italian, writing, and arithmetic. He was Jerolimo's colleague indeed, in that he was known for not paying his debts (Stutterheim).

1879 Two cities of refuge for bankrupts (Stoett and Damsteegt, p. 147).

1893 The pin released a gate, and thus the load, on the wheelbarrow.

1899 That is, a little metal badge to show that the bearer had the right to haul fish (Stutterheim).

1904 Proverbial. Harrebomée, 3:371, has several variations; e.g., "He who is quick to believe is soon fooled."

1906 I take two lines here to translate Bredero's one, though I preserve Stutterheim's line numbers.

1912 I suspect that Bredero makes the pronoun referents unclear for the same reason that he has characters mention people the audience does not know, and will not come to know; because this makes the audience feel that it is overhearing real conversation. Presumably the interlocutors know who "he" is, just as Tryn knows whether or not the Jan she is angry at is the same as the Jan we know. The fact that she does not stop to explain to us that he is the same man, or that he is not, makes her wrath all the more realistic. See line 1252.

1925 See note, line 1879.

1929 That is, one of the barges which were pulled along the canals by tow-ropes, this one with the city of Utrecht as destination.

1946 Stutterheim suggests that since the clerk assumes that they'll be going to a tavern, the notary should probably be played as something of a drunkard, and that the same must be assumed of the sheriff, since when Geeraart seeks him the only question is which tavern to search first (lines 1966–68).

1954 At the stock exchange, bidders would be noticed at the slightest sign.

1967 See note, line 1946.

1984 That is, protestants. For the *Geusen*, see the Introduction.

1992 That is, a protestant hymnal.

1995 "The crime of injuring majesty," i.e., high treason.

1996 These towns were known early as protestant towns, having already declared for the Prince of Orange at the Dordrecht conference in 1572.

2011 Because of the traditional association of noses and penises, although what this has to do with what Balich has just said, probably only Joost knows.

2020 All inns.

2053 That is, mythological paintings, some of the characters in which would be clothed, some nude.

2057-58 Lucas van Leiden: 1494–1533; Albrecht Dürer: 1471–1528; Martin van Heemskerk: 1498–1574; Hans Holbein: 1497–1543; Baccio Bandinelli: 1493–1560.

2100 The reference is to the elders who lusted after the chaste Susanna in the apocryphal book of Susanna.

2223 Proverbial. See A. A. Verdenius, "Aanteekeningen ˅bij Breero's Kluchten," *Tijds., v. Ned. Taal en Let.* 49 (1930):310.

2227 That is, thieves to be hanged in their own doorways.

This is the first translation of G. A. Bredero's **Spaanschen Brabander** (1617), perhaps the most beloved play ever written in the Netherlands. The work embodies the essence of early Amsterdam, a city ringing with talk, selling, and bawdry; a city whose river flows foul; a city stretching to accomodate a flood of immigration and an equal flood of controversy; a city where Dürers and Holbeins are sold as casually as eels and shoes; a city at once uneasy with and accepting of its startling diversity. Bredero sketches a halt-legged beadle, beggars, gabby old men, a fop, marble-playing boys, a roguish servant lad, hacklers, spinsters, prostitutes, junk dealers, widows, bakers, and bankrupts. He mounts upon the stage the same kind of breathing verisimilitude found in the canvases of Frans Hals and Jan Steen.

Professor Brumble's introduction outlines Bredero's career, discusses the dialects used in the play, sets the work in its historical and social context, and offers a critical analysis. His translation is based on the excellent edition of C. F. P. Stutterheim, *G. A. Bredero's Spaanschen Brabander* (Culemborg, 1974).

H. David Brumble III, Associate Professor of English at the University of Pittsburgh, has published articles on John Donne, Dante, Bredero, Brueghel the Elder, and American Indian sacred material. He is the author of *An Annotated Bibliography of American Indian and Eskimo Autobiographies* (1981) and a contributor to the forthcoming *Dictionary of the Bible and Biblical Tradition in English Literature.*

ɱ ʀ t s

meðieval & ʀenaissance texts & stuðies
is the publishing program of the
Center for Medieval and Early Renaissance Studies
at the State University of New York at Binghamton.

ɱʀts aims to provide the highest quality scholarship
in attractive and durable format at modest cost.